Voices from Furman University's LGBTQIA+ Community

Edited by A. Scott Henderson

Greenville, S.C.

Colors of the Rainbow

Voices from Furman University's LGBTQIA+ Community

Note: The opinions expressed in these pages are those of the contributors and do not necessarily reflect the views of Furman University.

An earlier version of "Gay 101" was published online in *Exquisite Pandemic* (December 2020).

Published by:

FpS

An imprint of United Writers Press

1175 Woods Crossing Rd., #2
Greenville, S.C. 29607
864-675-0540
www.fiction-addiction.com

ISBN: 978-1-952248-58-0

Cover & Book Design by Vally Sharpe of United Writers Press.

Printed in the United States of America.

For all those throughout history
who had to remain silent

Colors of the Rainbow

Introduction – A. Scott Henderson vii

1 **Loved Enough**
Elizabeth Allen 1

2 **Thoughts on Today**
Trevor Beeson 5

3 **This Pill**
Rob Cain 7

4 **Well, How Long Do You Have?**
Rob Cain 9

5 **Transparent**
K. C. Cox 11

6 **Both Ways**
Caroline Davis 12

7 **words spilled out on a piece of paper**
liv fletcher 13

8 **The Last Breath of August**
Mark Allan Gunnells 14

9 **Furman's Pathways**
Kelsey Hample 21

10 **A Queer Person's Field Guide to An Aviary**
Benjamin K. Haywood 25

11 **Conversion Camp**
A. Scott Henderson 41

12 **By the Numbers**
A. Scott Henderson 46

13 **Dating the Dead**
A. Scott Henderson 47

14 **Imposter Syndrome**
Riley Hughes 54

15 **Caryatids**
Kevin Kao 56

16 **Hubris (Rome)**
Kevin Kao 57

17 **Gay 101**
Nicholas Radel 58

18 **What You Never Know**
Nicholas Radel 63

19 **Honk For Jesus**
Roger Sneed 71

20 **MUNA Gets It**
Brandon Tensley 76

21 **Four Engines**
Claire Whitehurst 78

22 **Self-Portrait (An Echo)**
Claire Whitehurst 79

23 **Marching OUT in 1993**
Judith Williams 80

Contributors 87

Acknowledgments 91

Introduction

A. Scott Henderson

All communities derive strength from common bonds. Furman's LGBTQIA+ community is no exception. The initials LGBTQIA (lesbian, gay, bisexual, transgender, Queer, intersex, and asexual)—along with the plus sign—represent ties based on sexual orientation and gender expression. This anthology celebrates the people who proudly embrace those ties.

Even still, the selections in this volume describe the frequent challenges associated with being one's authentic self. This is especially true in the Bible Belt, a region where many of this anthology's contributors were born and raised. Indeed, Christian fundamentalism has been historically hostile toward LGBTQIA+ people. Moreover, the tension between spirituality and sexuality/gender can seemingly pose either/or dilemmas, dilemmas that cis-gender heterosexuals rarely encounter.

LGBTQIA+ individuals who decide to come out also have to consider the reactions of unsupportive family members. Not surprising, contributors allude to these apprehensions and to broader notions of what "family" means in the following pages.

Generational change and continuity are additional themes in this anthology. Some contributors recall events that occurred more than five decades ago. For them, the arrest and imprisonment of LGBTQIA+ individuals, New Right politics, the AIDS epidemic, Circuit/White Parties (large dance events), and the heyday of gay/lesbian bars are not just Wikipedia entries; they are facets of LGBTQIA+ history that can be reconstructed through personal stories or recast into fictional settings. On the other hand, a younger generation has come of age during an era characterized by demands for greater LGBTQIA+ rights, re-appropriation of the word "Queer," and efforts by elected officials to impose new restrictions on sexual/gender minority groups. These experiences—from gray-haired dating woes to monkeypox vaccinations, from disco songs to transgender equality—are all important aspects of LGBTQIA+ identities.

This volume's contributors raise important questions, too. How does popular culture conceptualize and depict the lives of LGBTQIA+ individuals? What are the affinities between LGBTQIA+ identities and the natural world? How can we document and memorialize the history of LGBTQIA+ communities? Are we obligated to speak out when we hear LGBTQIA+ slurs? How do we regain the things we have lost—or continue to move forward without them? These questions are examined through a variety of lenses—analytical, fictive, poetic, artistic, introspective, and whimsical. Contributors offer answers that are both enlightening and evocative.

If emotions can be conveyed through movement, then these selections are a dance, a dance of hard-earned joy. The words and images that fill these pages are testaments to resilience and determination, refusals to give up or give in. Above all else, they depict a community that has abandoned fear, replacing it with courage, hope, and affirmation. We invite readers to join in that dance.

Openness may not completely disarm prejudice,
but it's a good place to start.

– Jason Collins –

If I wait for someone else to validate my existence,
it will mean I'm shortchanging myself.

– Zanele Muholi –

I've been embraced by a new community.
That's what happens when you're finally honest about
who you are; you find others like you.

– Chaz Bono –

Loved Enough

Elizabeth Allen

The following was originally presented on July 7th, 2022, at Trinity Lutheran Church in Greenville, South Carolina.

On July 5th, 1998, twenty-four years and two days ago, I was baptized in this church by Pastor Bob Coon. I felt that this church, this congregation, these people were the very definition of home. Many wonderful people, some of you here this evening, helped me call this place my own. You were there to ask about my week, chatted with me about school, and answered my phone calls when I pleaded for you to buy some band fruit. I wanted to be the ideal pastor's daughter. I was in the youth group, participated and volunteered with Vacation Bible School, and went to church service every week. I loved being here in this place.

When I was younger, I was the loud and excited kid on the church playground. But as I grew up, I discovered that being the loud and excitable kid made me annoying and pretty weird. Plagued by undiagnosed anxiety, I edited my personality in an attempt to fit into the mold that some in this congregation expected. Snide comments helped motivate this misguided journey to reinvent myself.

But this self-editing was often painful. When someone complimented the fashionable Lilly Pulitzer dresses I wore to church, I felt like I was lying about who I was.

When girls gossiped about which boy was the cutest, I did my best to smile and nod like I knew what was going on.

When someone mentioned how skinny I was, I held back the snarky response of, "I'm struggling with an eating disorder."

When a family friend told me not to watch "The Ellen Show" because it would turn me gay, I kept my mouth shut and left her home early to watch the day's episode with my dad.

When my Sunday School teacher told us that "choosing to be gay" was a sin, I argued back. And when a youth group member told me to "Just go and kill yourself," I held back my tears until I was behind a pillar in the sanctuary to cry.

I kept lying to those around me about who I was to protect the little gay kid inside me who wanted to fit in so badly she would change everything about herself.

Even with all that lying, I was still too loud, too weird, too gay, too much.

The church was my safe place as a kid, but somewhere along the way it began to feel unsafe. I was never condemned from the pulpit or kicked out for being gay. My experience was much more subtle—I confronted discrimination that comes in the form of silence and exclusion.

While I had come to understand my sexuality by my sophomore year of high school, I didn't tell anyone about it until I graduated in 2016. Before announcing it to the whole world and being officially "out and about," my mom and I made a list of people in our lives who should know before Instagram did. First, we met with members of Trinity's staff. I was blown away by their kindness, care, affirmation, and compassion. I then called church members who we thought would be supportive, and Mom took the ones we were less sure about. Almost all of my phone calls went well, with Trinity members congratulating me and reminding me that I am loved just as I am. People went out of their way in those conversations to make sure I knew that I was a beloved part of this community of faith.

I learned that sometimes it's the people to whom we are related by the waters of baptism instead of the people we are related to by blood who can make the biggest differences in our lives.

While I was lucky, my mother bore the brunt of the non-affirming members.

These people, friends in and outside of church, hurled the most painful insults. They told her how I was an abomination. They told her that if she had stayed home with me, I wouldn't have turned out gay. They told her that since she had raised a gay daughter, maybe she wasn't fit to lead this congregation. Of course, that last assertion was utterly ridiculous—my mother is a confident, kick-ass advocate who would do anything to protect the people and congregation she loves.

I was thankful for my first year at college when I could escape Trinity and its members who thought I was an abomination. I ran away from everyone here, the good people who loved me unconditionally and those whose expectations I could never meet. I packed up the inclusive God I know and took that God to school with me. Once there, I got to be my loud, weird, gay self as much as I wanted to be. The belonging I had worked so hard for at Trinity was easily found at Furman.

As non-affirming families left Trinity and found new church homes, I felt that my coming out had led to a mass exodus of people whom I'd once loved. I thought I was responsible for the entire split Trinity was going through to become an inclusive and open space, that I was making people choose because I had decided to be my true self. Despite the love and compassion that was shown to me by some members, I wondered if I should have taken that one member's advice and kept my sexuality a secret forever.

But the direction in which Trinity has gone is not just because of me. There are many like-minded people who are ready to fight for my rights and the rights of others in the Queer community. Trinity moved to celebrate same-sex marriage in May of 2017 because a committee of church members met, researched, and discussed the Lutheran interpretation of scripture. My little gay self didn't make that decision. This congregation worked together to create a path for where we are now, a genuinely safe space.

I feel safe here in this place again. I can see and celebrate those close to me who started coming to Trinity years before I was born. I see many new people looking for a similar sense of peace—the same acceptance that embraces me every time I come through these doors, whether it's the three red ones on Main Street or the humble gym doors.

I am so grateful that Trinity is a place where I even forget that my sexuality is a big deal to some people. If you've spoken to me, you know I would much rather talk about Starbursts, my classroom, guinea pigs, or what liquid you would fill a bathtub with. At Trinity, I can now just be me, not worrying about conforming to anybody else's expectations.

While I was hurt and bullied by people who once called this congregation home, I never thought God hated me. In the reading tonight, God says, "you are precious and honored in my sight, and I love you." When we fall short, God is always there, loving us unconditionally. When governments and organized religion and angry internet trolls make you feel anything less than perfect, God is still there, loving you when it feels like no one else does.

God made every single one of us exactly how we are. God made me to be loud enough, weird enough, gay enough, and as it turns out, loved enough. We are all enough for God.

Thanks be to God. *Amen.*

Thoughts on Today

Trevor Beeson

An email from a son to his parents in response to a homophobic sermon watched together during the Covid lockdown.

Mom & Dad:

I know what happened today may seem a bit dramatic to you. What I want you to know is that these are emotions I have been dealing with for a long time. I have mostly held them in and kept them from you because I don't want you to know how much I hurt. I don't ever want to do or say anything I might regret, so my first instinct is always to escape. That's why I left the lake house today.

I also want you to know that I love you—and that I know you love me. I'm your son and you're my parents and nothing is going to change that. But I don't have the same beliefs or theology that you or my siblings do. Those beliefs are deeply hurtful to me. I am not saying this to make you feel guilty or to ask you to change your own beliefs. I certainly wouldn't want you to ask that of me. I just can't keep my feelings hidden any longer.

I know the natural response is the desire to do something. The most I ask is that you respect my views—and to realize that my beliefs won't stop me from loving you or from being a Christian. Deep down I crave your affirmation and celebration of who I am as a gay man, but I am also coming to terms with the fact that that probably won't happen. That's a lot for me to bear right now.

We have different understandings of the Bible and sexuality. Your beliefs are held by millions. My beliefs are held by millions. And that is okay. I appreciate the way you have raised me and helped me to become who I am today. In fact, I embrace the majority of values and morals you instilled in me. However, the things we disagree on are central to my identity and my very personhood. I know you might not think sexuality is an integral part of one's identity, but I do.

Your beliefs are always in the back of my mind, but today those beliefs were so blatantly in my face that I couldn't ignore them or keep my reaction stuffed down inside me. Even though I feel wounded, please understand that I'm not going anywhere. I just need more time and more space to cope, to learn, and to grow.

Love,
Trevor

This Pill

Rob Cain

It is just a pill.

I had to fly to a liberal city to take the first one. I couldn't do it in my hometown. Not within a five-minute drive of my family members. Not one and a half miles from the church that taught me to hate who I am. Swallowing that PreP[1] pill means I swallow any chance of ever denying I am a gay man. This pill is like crossing the Rubicon—it means that I admit to having sex with other men. This pill is something I'm worried my parents might see on their insurance statement. This pill is just a pill. This pill couldn't possibly be more than a pill. This pill is absolutely more than a pill. This pill is everything.

My friend Caroline counts down: five-four-three-two-one. I swallow the pill with a gulp of iced coffee.

I don't have to die anymore. I'm reborn when I swallow this pill. The next day I take the pill with a Coke Zero. The time after that I take it with a man I slept with as he takes his alongside me. And the next time I take the pill I'm in New York City, my soon to be home, visiting friends. This is freedom. This pill is freedom.

This pill is also gratitude, gratitude for all the doctors and researchers who are saving thousands of lives. This pill is history. It's remembering my uncles telling me the stories of their friends dying left and right of HIV.

---

[1] **PreP (Pre-Exposure Prophylaxis) refers to a medication or combination of medications taken to prevent the spread of HIV (Human Immunodeficiency Virus).*

It's my uncles waking up every day wondering why they aren't dead. It's refusing to forget an entire generation of Queer folks wiped out while the government sat idly by. This (free) pill is reparations. This pill is dissent.

This pill isn't just another pill.

This pill is everything.

Well, How Long Do You Have?

Rob Cain

I got my monkeypox vaccination today. I am in the Northeast and this vaccine is only widely available in liberal states and large cities. Not in my hometown. Why is this the case? Well, how long do you have?

I got my monkeypox vaccination today. The nurses were encouraging and kind. They were TB & STI nurses. There was fun music playing and I felt happy to be myself. I asked why this disease was more common among men who have sex with men. The nurse responded, "Oh, you mean for folks who don't have normal sex?" She quickly recovered by explaining she didn't mean it that way—she just wasn't sure about the correct language to use. She wasn't being malicious, so it shouldn't hurt my feelings, right? Well, how long do you have?

I got my monkeypox vaccination today. I texted a photo of my vaccination card to all my friends. I'm proud of myself and they're proud of me. I didn't text anyone in my family. Why didn't I text them? Well, how long do you have?

I got my monkeypox vaccination today. I've been spending the week in Upstate New York with my best friend's family. They are kind and inclusive, allowing me to be who I am. They affirm their gender non-conforming child who is engaged to a transitioning male. The things that are said and left unsaid in this home are balms to my soul. Why does it affect me so much and make me feel so at peace? Well, how long do you have?

I got my monkeypox vaccination today. Maybe this is a small taste of what an older generation felt during the AIDS epidemic. Perhaps this will be different. I got my shot in a clinic inside of an old church. How did *that* feel?

Well, how long do you have?

Transparent

K. C. Cox

What you see is who I am,
and I am what you see,
seeing myself as a boy—and then a man
ever since I was five.

At that innocent age I would ask,
Why don't I look like Dad?
All I wanted to do was to
"shave, shave" like him.

When I was older, there was no greater gift
than giving birth to my children—
to mother them was a gift,
to father them was a gift.

Being a transparent is a gift,
what you see is what you get,
a true heart—loving, hoping, understanding,
always by your side no matter what.

I walk in faith stronger
than I have ever been,
feeling, knowing, reminding others
that I'll always care.

Both Ways

Caroline Davis

That's not who you are.
Just pick a team.
You can't
Live your life
Straddling a fence.
It isn't
The way you're supposed to be.
You're absolutely
Selfish and greedy.
Erasing whole identities for the convenience of others is
How the game is played.
This doesn't have to be
Part of you.
This is all
A phase.
It's not
Something I can understand.
Feeling a little different is
Unsafe here.
You will never be
Accepted as you are.
It's easier to be
A vision of something you are not.
You don't ever have to be
The one without community.
That's not who you are.

[Now, read from the bottom up.]

words spilled out on a piece of paper

liv fletcher

somedays i love being queer
i love seeing the world through a different lens
i love the feeling of connecting with another queer person
when we can share our stories, whether they are filled with love or rage, in complete safety
i love the feeling of acceptance when i finally get the courage to open up
i love the excitement of realizing we both like each other more than just "friends"

but then there are days where i don't love being queer
when seeing the world differently feels isolating instead of electrifying
when the stories you have to share are more traumatic than they are hopeful
when your biggest fear was that they wouldn't show up to your wedding
so you felt a sense of relief when they passed
when your story isn't taken seriously because only men are capable of such evil

i hope that one day our perspectives will be seen as a gift
that the stories we tell will be more light than they are dark
that "coming out" won't be a prerequisite to telling people who you like
that when our relationships are seen as sexual, it's not solely through the eyes of men
and when they take our relationships seriously, they're seen not just as sunshine and rainbows

The Last Breath of August

Mark Allan Gunnells

Are you the Andy Phelps who wrote The Last Breath of August?

Anderson sat at the computer, staring at the strange Facebook message with a frown. The sender, a Michael Hutchinson, was not anyone Anderson was connected with on social media, and unless Anderson accepted the message request, Michael would never even know Anderson had read it.

After looking over the one-sentence message a final time, Anderson shook his head and logged out of Facebook without accepting the message request.

> *Sorry to be a pest, but I just read* Last Breath of August *and it is my new favorite book. I can't find much information about the writer, and he never seemed to publish anything else. I found a few other Andy Phelps on here, but you're the only one who lives in South Carolina, which is where the book was set. If I have the wrong person, let me know and I won't bother you anymore.*

Anderson was in line at Starbucks when he read this second message on his phone. He put the phone away and ordered his drink and a muffin, trying not to think about the messages, but unable to think of anything else. Sitting at a table in the corner, he pulled up Amazon and searched for *The Last Breath of August*.

The book was released back in 1991 and was long out of print. There were a few used copies going for mere pennies from second-party sellers, and the book had a total of seventeen reviews. Anderson scrolled through them. Most were middle-of-the-road three-star reviews, a couple of one-star reviews that complained the book was too boring, one that said it was an evil book and should be burned. The most recent review, posted only a week prior, consisted of a single word: "Brilliant!" The reviewer was listed as MHutch.

> *On the off chance you are the Andy Phelps who wrote* The Last Breath of August, *I just want to share how profoundly the book impacted me. I'm about to start my senior year of high school and I live in a tiny little town in Texas. I've never exactly fit in. Not at school, not at home, not anywhere. It may be 2022 in the rest of the world, but my family and my town seem to be lagging a few decades behind. The effeminate bookish kid still stands out in all the wrong ways around here. Anyway, I was in Goodwill last week, just looking at the books they had for fifty cents. If you've ever been in a Goodwill, you know their book selection consists mostly of Danielle Steel and Stephen King and Jackie Collins and John Grisham. I'm not sure what made me stop on your book (if it is your book), but when I pulled out the tattered paperback, the cover really caught my eye. It shows two guys sitting at the end of a pier with their backs to the viewer, leaning toward each other so that their shoulders just slightly touch. Not super suggestive or anything, but kind of intimate. I bought it and ended up tearing through it in only a couple of days. I know this may sound silly, but the story made me feel seen. The relationship between the two main characters was romantic without being oversexualized. It was actually kind of sweet and innocent. Mostly what drew me in, though, was the depiction of a gay kid growing up in a place where everything and everyone around him is telling him he's wrong, that he's broken in some way, but even in this environment he*

finds some self-acceptance and self-love. That is something I've struggled with, but even though this is just a book, I feel like it has provided me with some strength and confidence. It makes me feel a little less alone.

"Hey."

Anderson started, then quickly minimized Facebook on the computer, bringing back up the spreadsheet full of numbers. "Hey Dave, what's up?"

Dave Roberts shared the next cubicle over and was standing to peer over the partition wall. He did that a lot. Anderson hated it, another reason he wished he had an actual office, but he was too polite to say anything.

"Did you see the email from home office?" Dave asked.

"No, must have missed it."

"They said they've been tracking our lunch punches and the average worker is exceeding the allotted lunch break by five minutes. Can you believe that? I guess Big Brother really is...hey, Andy, you okay?"

Anderson also hated being called Andy, but again he was too polite to say anything. "Yeah, I'm fine. Why?"

"Your eyes are all red and watery."

Anderson swiped at his eyes. "Summer allergies, you know. I need to take some Zyrtec."

"Yeah, for me it's worse in spring when the pollen first starts getting so bad."

Dave went on for a while, but Anderson mostly tuned him out, listening peripherally so he could grunt or nod in the right places. When Dave finally ducked back down, Anderson pulled up Facebook again and reread the message. But he still didn't accept it.

I discovered a blog that focuses on "obscure and undiscovered authors." A few years ago, they did an entry all about Andy Phelps. Actually, they had little information about the man himself, but a great deal about The Last Breath of August *and its publication. Turns out when the book came out in the early 90s, having a book with teenage protagonists that dealt frankly with themes of homosexuality and attraction was an even bigger no-no than it is now. At least now we have things like* Heartstopper *and* Simon vs. the Homo Sapiens Agenda *and* Boy Meets Boy. *At the time there was nothing in the YA landscape like that, and people apparently lost their shit. There were protests and threats, the book was banned from libraries and bookstores across the country. The blogger says Phelps and the publisher were almost slapped with pornography charges, even though there were no actual sex scenes in the book. Seems like Phelps just disappeared after that. Not sure if no other publisher would touch him or he simply stopped writing, or both. Anyway, I'm not sure if my messages are getting through or if this is even the right person, but if so, I wanted to say that your book still exists out there, and it found its target audience in me. I've heard about people saying they read some book that changed their lives, but this is the first time I've ever experienced it. So Andy Phelps, wherever you are...thank you.*

Anderson climbed the ladder into his attic. There wasn't room to fully stand, so he crouched low and crab-walked to the far corner and the mildewed boxes that held all the detritus of a life that was no longer needed but felt too important somehow to toss out.

He dug through action figures, children's picture books, photo albums, articles of clothing kept less for style than for significance of when they were worn (the bow-tie he wore to his prom, the shirt he wore the first day of college, the jeans he wore the night he lost his virginity). It was in the third box he opened that he found what he was looking for.

A paperback book. The pages were yellowed with age, but the spine intact. An old book, but one that had never been read. On the cover was the image of the two young men, shoulders touching. Above them in a misty font, the title: *The Last Breath of August*. Below them: *A novel of self-discovery* by Andy Phelps.

Anderson let himself fall back onto his butt, heedless of the dust, and cracked open the book to the first page. By the light streaming into the large circular window behind him, he began to read. Words that felt unfamiliar to him, written by a man who now seemed like a stranger.

> *I guess this will be my last message. Either you aren't the writer of* The Last Breath of August, *or you aren't reading these messages at all. Regardless, I'll always be grateful I found this book in Goodwill. I actually gave it to my mother to read. She came to me last night, telling me she'd finished it and asking if there was anything I wanted to talk about. I didn't come out to her, I don't feel like I'm quite ready for that yet, but she opened the door for me. And now I can imagine stepping through it without my world imploding. I may have gotten here eventually all on my own, but this book helped. It helped a lot. Wherever Andy Phelps is out in the world, thank you. You're a life-saver.*

Anderson hesitated on the front stoop for a moment, then rang the bell. He felt nervous, like a teenager picking up a date for the first time. When the door opened, Anderson tensed. The man who appeared in the doorway wasn't the one he'd been expecting, but still Anderson knew who it must be.

"Kenny?" Anderson said.

The man looked stunned, as if he'd opened the door to find a leprechaun standing there with a pot of gold. "Um, yeah. A.J.?"

"I prefer to go by Anderson."

"Nice to meet you. Feels strange to say that after all these years, and I've heard so much about you I feel like I know you, but..."

"But we've never actually met," Anderson said. "I know, that's my fault and I apologize. Is my father home by any chance?"

As if on cue, from somewhere behind Kenny a familiar voice called out, "Who's at the door? If it's another of those girls peddling cookies tell her that a dozen boxes is our limit."

And then Anderson's father was there in the doorway, standing next to his husband. If Kenny had looked stunned, Anderson's father looked absolutely gut-punched. "A.J. What are you doing here?"

Before Anderson could answer, a whistling arose deep in the house. Kenny said, "Excuse me, the water is ready for the tea," then disappeared, leaving Anderson and his father staring at each other across the threshold.

"You've never just dropped in before," his father said after a moment. "What brings you to the neighborhood?"

In answer, Anderson held up the paperback in his hand. "I finally read your book. Only took me a couple of decades, but I finally got to it."

His father took the book and absently flipped it open to the dedication page. "To my son, Andy Jr. I hope someday you can understand."

"What did you think?" his father asked in a tentative voice, as if bracing himself for a critical assault.

"It was beautiful. Truly, Dad, I thought it was an exceptional story."

His father's lips twitched, trying to form a smile, but hesitant to commit. "That means a lot coming from you."

"Look, I know that I haven't exactly been a good son."

His father held up a hand and said, "We don't have to rehash this."

"No, I need to say this. I didn't handle it well when you and Mom divorced. Then when you came out and published this book...well, I was a teenager and I found the whole thing so mortifying. All the kids at school knowing I had a gay dad, the guys in the locker room asking if it ran in the family. I felt like your coming out was a personal attack on me. I never thought about what you were going through, what it was like for you. And then I grew up and I still didn't think about any of that. I held onto this useless sense of betrayal as if it were real. I came by today to let you know I realize now how selfish and stupid I've been. I know at this point we don't really know each other, but after reading your book, I feel like I have gotten to know you a little bit. And I want to get to know you more, you and Kenny. And let you get to know me. If you want."

At first his father didn't speak, but the tears in his eyes said it all. He nodded vigorously and stepped aside. "Come in. Have some tea with us."

As Anderson stepped into his father's home for the first time, he pulled out his phone. "Hey Dad, I know you aren't on social media, but there's something from Facebook I have to show you."

And then the door shut behind them.

Furman's Pathways

Kelsey Hample

It was my first year, my first semester, as a professor at Furman University. I was walking between Riley Hall and the Trone Center alongside the library—a pathway I have become quite familiar with in the five years since, as it leads from my office toward the Dining Hall for lunch. The walkway is cobbled in brick and has a gentle curve to it. As someone who prefers to walk quickly and arrive on time, I have noticed that this particular pathway is not designed for efficient travel. It's designed for something else—maybe for aesthetics or for slower walks with pleasant conversations.

"I was worried that these sweatpants make me look dyke-y."

"Oh, no! You look fine..."

This was the pleasant conversation that reached my ears on that path during my first fall at Furman. A concern shared between two female-presenting students, who I guessed were first-years based on their matching Furman t-shirts.

I didn't stop them or say anything. I was shocked and silent, my mind spinning with possibilities. I was tempted to ask whether *I* looked "dyke-y" in my slacks—or maybe introduce myself as a "dyke" in order to shock and silence *them*. On the other hand, I wanted to have a productive exchange, though I didn't know how to start it. Plus, I had somewhere to be, and they had the right to freedom of thought and expression. They continued walking past me, and I continued walking past them. But I have felt stuck to that moment and place long since then.

I kept walking that pathway, lunch after lunch. I settled into work and life at Furman, unpacking my books and sharing dinners with welcoming and supportive colleagues. On one of those evenings, I recounted my experience on that path. A colleague assured me not to worry, that I would soon have the confidence to intervene as I got used to my place in the Furman community. I understood the point, but even halfway into my second gin I knew it was more complicated than that.

I've revisited and retraced that pathway many times, trying to understand my inaction. How could I have been so powerless around those students? My power should have come through the hierarchy of our positions: I was a professor, albeit an assistant professor, and they were students. Probably even first-year students. But their power to knock the voice out of me with one word came from the institution of heteronormativity. From the social acceptance of anti-Queer jokes and casual slurs.

I follow a turn in the pathway. Was I silent because "dyke-y" wasn't strong enough to warrant my intervention? I've never identified as lesbian—the word just feels pejorative to me. I've heard the same thing from other Queer women in my generation. If the students had used a slur against gay men—a slur I'm uncomfortable even typing—would I have been moved to intervene? Why is "dyke" easier for me to type than "faggot"? Have I internalized enough misogyny that I accept "dyke-y" as a descriptor rather than a slur? That I'm not bothered when women—from so-called "sluts" to prudes—are defined by their sexual behavior?

Now I feel like I've gone too far. What do I really know about internalized misogyny? Maybe it would have been totally out of line for me to have intervened in that conversation. Furman is my community, but it belongs to those students as well. Should I have the right to impose censorship to avoid personal discomfort, or should people have the right to privacy on that path? And those students didn't know who I was. I wasn't even wearing baggy sweatpants.

I've been on this walk before. Many times. I'm always passing, unintentionally. It is a privilege in a heteronormative society to be able to pass as heterosexual. I can usually determine if and when to "come out." I get to avoid the penalties that many members of underrepresented groups encounter. I don't face threats, I'm not (always) underestimated or overlooked, I'm not considered too aggressive or "just a bad fit for us." Was I simply choosing to exercise my passing privilege by not outing myself to those students?

As I retrace the steps, I think about how this pathway was built. I have a quirk, which is that I love to pay taxes. Really. You can build a road (or path) with taxes collected throughout the community, or through private funds and fences; I prefer the former. I feel differently, though, about minority taxes—the uncompensated work that minority group members perform to improve their workplaces and communities. I've been impressed by stories of Furman's pioneering female faculty members and black students, transgender staff, and others who overcame the challenge of finding their voices—the voice I couldn't find on that sidewalk—and who often went on to pay additional taxes to improve our communities and figurative pathways.

I've arrived at a crossroads. I am grateful for the minority taxes that people paid before me, but I still find myself opting to pass much of the time. Sure, I do some extra committee work, but I'm not a living example as my predecessors were and are. I've heard from recent graduates that there are many Queer Furman students who choose to stay closeted. Could I be a better example to those students by being a role model of a successful Queer person? A Queer person who walks safely through her community? A "dyke" who doesn't wear baggy sweatpants?

I zoom out. I zoom out to see the whole pathway, the whole campus, the whole world. Have I really been lost in thought retracing this insignificant pathway while Queer people around the country and globe are denied jobs, disowned, imprisoned, beaten, raped, murdered? I am in a position of relative power at an institution that, since my first semester on that path, has demonstrated part of its support for Queer community members through launching the "Out at Furman" webpage, a webpage that I am not too intimidated to be featured on. But what else am I doing for my broader community from my place of comfort? How can I spill ink about the mention of "dyke-y" sweatpants when I haven't devoted more time and energy to strengthening my global Queer community by working for safety and equity?

I rest at a bench along that Furman pathway. I do want to invest more in my global community, but I also need to take action in my local community where I can have the biggest impact. As I write this in 2022, I can't help wondering whether my right to marry a same-sex partner is at risk of being taken away. In some ways, I take for granted that those two students would not have said the word "dyke" in a classroom—that they know the word is (at a minimum) impolite and therefore shouldn't be used in most settings. I shouldn't take that for granted and I shouldn't stop at ensuring that academic spaces are inclusive and respectful. We need the pathways, too.

A Queer Person's Field Guide to An Aviary

Benjamin K. Haywood

Preface

As a closeted gay kid in the rural American South, I didn't always feel like I belonged in the spaces of everyday life that engulfed me—the ballparks, classrooms, and churches of my youth. Fortunately, my parents never forced me to fit the mold prescribed in those spaces and instead celebrated and encouraged my unique interests and passions. First to take note of my deep connection to the natural world, they found every opportunity they could to cultivate it. As luck would have it, just a few short miles up the road from my hometown was the young and burgeoning North Carolina Zoo. Although the North Carolina Zoo officially started in the late 1970s, the grand opening of five original major habitats occurred in the summer of 1980, just a few short years before my birth.

Because I was a child of the early 1980s and living only a short distance from the fledgling zoo, you might say I grew up with and in that place. The North Carolina Zoo became a home away from home for me and my family in the first decade of its existence and has remained so ever since. The sights and sounds of the initial African-themed exhibits—the lions, zebra, and giraffe—are still some of the most vivid memories of my childhood—and some of the happiest. Those experiences provided the formative interactions with wild creatures that cultivated a life-long passion for conservation of wildlife and wild places.

One of the very first exhibits was the R.J. Reynolds Forest Aviary, which opened at the nascent North Carolina Zoo in the early 1980s. It was and will always be my favorite place at the zoo. As a child, the sights, sounds, and immersive experience the facility provided allowed me and my rural North Carolina family the opportunity to leave our world momentarily and emerge in a tropical forest across the globe, surrounded by altogether captivating plants and animals. Since that time, and despite having lived in a variety of places far away from the zoo, my trips "home" often include a visit to this avian paradise. Even today, I can trace every corner of the facility in my mind's eye, with memories of each bird species present over the years fluttering by as I walk through. It is no exaggeration that my lifelong love of birds began in that very space—no other place can conjure the feeling of serenity that I get when I step into the building.

It was not until I was much older that I realized the significance of the aviary in my personal journey as a gay man. There were important, critical lessons I absorbed from the experiences and interactions in that space that I had no way of knowing I needed as a young person wrestling with my sexuality—and wrestling with how it intersected with family, faith, and the broader community. Unbeknownst to me, the deep wisdom I obtained in that lush garden fertilized a future path of acceptance and hope. This short Queer field guide to the aviary is thus a homage to a sacred space and a commemoration of the many affirming, encouraging, and life-giving lessons that it can teach. It is a celebration of birds, wildness, and Queerness, written with the hope that our winged companions speak to my Queer comrades as much as they have to me.

A Note on Species Conservation Status: The International Union for Conservation of Nature (IUCN) conservation status of each species featured in this guide is noted at its first appearance. These categories indicate whether a species still exists (at all and/or in the wild) and how likely the species is to become extinct in the near future. Birds classified in three of the nine IUCN categories are included in this guide, as noted below:

* Least Concern: At lowest risk, plentiful in the wild
** Near Threatened: Likely to become endangered in the near future
*** Critically Endangered: At extremely high risk of extinction in the wild

Stop One: Four-Feet Flamingos

Once you make your way to the heart of the natural-habitat zoo, before entering the aviary building, you will be greeted first by the sounds (and smells!) of the Chilean Flamingo.** Located in an open-air habitat right outside the main aviary entrance, the flock of nearly thirty birds has a noticeable shrimpy odor, accompanied by the muted grunts they use to communicate with each other. These South American birds are a reminder that the world extends far beyond the limited perspectives of our natal, sometimes close-minded communities. Found in shallow lakes and lagoons from the high Andes all the way to Patagonia, they can stand up to four feet tall, with subdued but elegant pink- and salmon-colored feathers.

Traversing vast coastal plains with expansive horizons and opportunities, the Chilean Flamingo knows the value of standing tall and proud in any setting or circumstance. Their frequent-flier status exposes them to a wide variety of places, people, and cultures—the broad diversity of life that is essential for healthy and thriving social and ecological communities. Keep your head up, they nod, as you navigate your path. Think beyond your present circumstances. It might feel like your world is limited and constrained sometimes, but it is much bigger than you think. Despite fervid voices that suggest otherwise, there is plenty of room for you on this vast blue planet, too.

Stop Two: The Regal Pigeon

Stepping into the aviary proper affords a sudden and overwhelming opportunity to belie space and time and immerse yourself into a lush, tropical forest. Often one of the most notable and immediately visible birds in this vast jungle is the Victoria Crowned Pigeon,** which you might see on the ground, where it typically forges for fallen fruit. Aside from its size (it is the largest pigeon in the world), take note of the grand, fan-shaped crest of lacy feathers perched atop its head. Named after Britain's Queen Victoria, both the males and females possess these crowns. In particular, males work to ensure they maintain elegant and ornate crown feathers in order to attract potential mates. Native to the island of New Guinea, Victoria Crowned Pigeons are a bit unusual in the bird world, containing sixteen feathers in their tail (instead of the customary twelve) and lacking an oil gland. Further still, like many birds, this species upends notions of traditional gendered beauty. Both males and females possess rich, striking blue-gray maroon plumage and elaborate accessory garments on their heads; male Victoria Crowned Pigeons are truly the drag "queens" (pun intended) of the avian world.

As someone who might feel a little different, too, let these birds provide comfort. With extra tail feathers, different anatomy, and lavish accoutrements, they break out of the standard avian mold. As you come into your own, may their unabashed nonconformity inspire you to find your way towards authentic expression. And for goodness' sake, wear whatever you damn well please on your head!

Stop Three: Treetop Timidity

As you meander down the main aviary path, look up for a moment and you might find another pigeon species quietly tucked along a hidden tree branch—the Nicobar Pigeon.** At first, you might just see a dark-blue underbelly, but watch carefully for the bird to move and you will catch a glimpse of a fantastic palette of vibrant colors. Nicobar Pigeons have long, trailing plumes extending from the neck in a variety of colors, from dark green, to gray, to blue, and even orange. These birds glisten like a rainbow just after a storm. The closest living relative to the Dodo, and native to dense forested offshore islands in southeastern Asia and Australia, these shy and secretive birds are not often seen in the wild due to their timid nature. However, they are frequently captured for the pet trade and caged for their elegance and beauty. To remain safe and secure, the Nicobar Pigeon has learned to roost high in trees, keeping a watchful eye on those below who might wish them harm. The kaleidoscopic plumage of the Nicobar Pigeon is most spectacular in this canopy space, where beams of sunlight penetrate the dense forest. Underneath the golden rays of sun, these birds bring a symbol of pride and diverse beauty—the rainbow—to life in the treetops.

Like a Nicobar tucked quietly on high, keep careful watch for both internal and external voices that might dampen your inner radiance. Rising above potential captors of their beauty, these birds know the importance of cultivating spaces and communities of safety and celebration, spaces that resist treatment as an oddity to be confined, controlled, scrutinized, or showcased as a spectacle of peculiarity. It might not always be easy, but keep climbing to find your light and remove those obstacles that dim it. Embrace your iridescence!

Stop Four: Eclectic Eclectus

Making your first major left turn into the heart of the aviary, you cannot miss one of the main attractions of the facility—the Eclectus Parrot.* A medium-sized bird, the Eclectus is unlike many parrots because it is sexually dimorphic, meaning males and females have different external appearances. In this case, the differences are stark, so much so that the first European ornithologists to encounter and classify them thought they were different species altogether. Males are bright green with a hint of blue and red on the wing and a yellow beak, while females are a rich burgundy with a deep violet belly and black beak. Most likely you will see the female in the aviary—and she will probably notice you as soon as you notice her. She might begin to fidget to ensure she can keep her eyes on you—and she might even bellow a loud screech to say hello. Unlike the muted pink of our flamingo friends and the mild blues of the Victoria Crowned Pigeon, the male and female Eclectus both sport bright, bold, unmistakable colors. Long used in decorations made by the indigenous communities in New Guinea, from which they hail, the vibrant feathers pop within the tropical forests where they live.

There are certainly times when life calls for the humble and mild, but the Eclectus commands fierce boldness, too. Yes, your sexual orientation is just one of many aspects of who you are, much like feather pigmentation is merely one element of what it means to be an Eclectus. But powerful forces intent on oppression and erasure have long sought to keep that one slice of the pinwheel of your identity suppressed and ignored. The Eclectus Parrot is a vivid example of why it is hard to ignore the loudest color in the room. Boldness warrants respect, and vibrancy, in all forms, adds to the spice of life. Do not let others rob you—or the Queer community to which you belong—of the bold celebrations of your unique, one-of-a-kind nature.

Stop Five: Coua Realness

If you pause for a moment to look beyond the vivid Eclectus Parrot, you might notice a bird known not for its plumage, but for its erratic behavior instead. Often described as "restless," the Crested Coua* is mostly a drab gray and cream-colored bird that rarely flies, but instead bounces sporadically from perch to perch among the trees in its native Madagascar home. A member of the cuckoo family, these birds are highly inquisitive and independent. They do not flock, but are found either alone or in pairs. Despite their overall monochromatic appearance, if you are lucky enough to see one up close you will notice its beautiful eyes, which are thanks to a turquoise-colored bare skin patch that surrounds them. If birds could sign modeling contracts, these ones would make a killing selling eye-liner! No need to fret, however, if you do not see this bird immediately. That is because it will not be long before you hear it. The Crested Coua is highly vocal, best known for its distinctive "laser gun" call comprised of a series of pierced, descending notes. These birds do not

follow the crowd by any stretch of the imagination, but instead regularly exhibit their own style, identity, and voice; you could certainly consider them the social influencers and trendsetters of the bird world.

You might feel pressure to conform as well, with voices from all directions ready to tell you precisely what it means to be Queer. You might be encouraged to check a box so that others can easily categorize you, or to obey an implied code of conduct that is simultaneously rigid and nebulous. Stereotypes abound in all directions. Thoughtfully consider the advice, counsel, perspectives, and experiences of others with grace. But, in the end, like the Coua, define yourself on your own terms. Your voice is unique. The world needs to hear it.

Stop Six: Sunny Disposition

Arriving in the center of the facility, you will soon stumble upon a small pool of water, with fallen logs and soggy soil patches nearby for many of the wetland species that live there. You might glimpse what looks like a miniature heron blending in with the brownish hue of the logs and standing very still. The Sunbittern* is an inconspicuous bird, camouflaged well against the earth tones of the lowland aquatic streams that it inhabits in much of central and northern South America. Not much larger than a crow, these birds have long legs, slender bodies, and sharp, pointy bills. The Sunbittern is a rather secretive species, walking carefully and quietly in search of food close to the ground. You would not know it from its unremarkable exterior feathers, but these

birds possess a secret weapon. Fierce defenders of their companions and young when threatened, they open their wings wide and fan out their tail feathers. In the center of each wing is a striking sunburst pattern of crimson, black, and white. When fanned out along with the tail, these noticeable patches look (from behind) like two large eyes emanating from what appears to be a formidable creature. All at once this small and timid bird transforms into a large, fierce foe via a carefully orchestrated bluff. The unassuming Sunbittern utilizes rich and vivid beauty hidden within its wings to protect itself and those it loves.

Even with progress, we still live in a world where expressing a non-majority sexual orientation might cause others to spew hate and disdain. Sadly, you have likely been targeted by unkind words such as "sinful," "hedonistic," "abomination," "unnatural," "perverse," and "evil." You know the stares, you recognize the avoidance, you have sensed the pious disapproval, and you understand what it feels like to live in fear that your sexual orientation might somehow prevent you from accessing basic rights and protections. When threatened by such small minds, take a cue from the Sunbittern and show the fantastic beauty you have within. Don't fight hate with hate—your inner beauty is your secret weapon.

Stop Seven: Whistled Wisdom

Just below and beyond the central water feature is a tranquil wading pool, perfect for the multiple duck species that call this tropical paradise home. One of them, the White-faced Whistling Duck,* is a striking bird, not easily missed when gliding atop the surface of the water. With a white and black head, a dark rufus chest, and a black belly and tail, this species is rather abundant in freshwater marshes and lakes throughout tropical regions in South America and Africa. Several features distinguish the White-face Whistling Duck from other duck species, making them an "odd duck out," so to speak. First, because males and females look identical, the males are not able to rely on the typically elaborate plumage common in other male ducks to attract a mate. Instead, males of this species invest far more energy in extending care and concern for potential mates through behavior—providing gifts or food, preening regularly, and defending a suitable habitat. It is not unusual for this species to form life-long monogamous pairs, sharing parenting roles equally and demonstrating incredible devotion to one another. Even more uncommon, the White-faced Whistling Duck is nocturnal, usually resting in flocks during the day and foraging through the night. Perhaps most peculiar for a duck, however, is the sound they make to communicate. Instead of the typical quack you might expect, they communicate via a series of high-pitched whistles! A whistling, nocturnal, perpetually monogamous duck is an absolute oddball among the family of birds (Anatidae) to which it belongs. I am willing to bet that the powerful majority at the annual Anatidae convention has long adopted a political platform designed to exclude and deny this species full membership in the group—to treat them like second-class citizens. After all, there is nothing "normal" about the White-faced Whistling Duck.

You might feel like an oddball at times too, especially in a world that celebrates masculinity, patriarchy, and intolerance. No doubt you know those who argue that your supposed abnormal nature prevents you from participating in the same types of relationships or customs that are common among heterosexuals. According to this logic, what matters above all else—above the need for companionship, touch, intimacy, loyalty, or love—is the reproductive anatomy of your partner. In spite of such discrimination, be sure of this—no matter the pitch of your voice, the colors in your wardrobe, or your daily routines and rhythms, just like the White-faced Whistling Duck you deserve life-long relationships (romantic and otherwise) that celebrate tenderness, respect, deep connection, and devotion. Do not let someone else's narrow perspective limit your possibilities or promise.

Stop Eight: Flock Together

Although a long rest in one of the benches by the wading pool might be tempting, there are more birds to be discovered in this miniature paradise. Just around the corner beyond the open water, you will find your eyes drawn toward brilliant concentrations of deep red color among the verdant green canopy. Scattered closely together in one of the large, towering trees in the exhibit is a small flock of Scarlet Ibis.* Named for the deep red feathers that cover their bodies, these medium-sized wading birds have long, curved black bills and thin pink legs and feet. Like flamingos, the red in their feathers comes from the carotene found in the crustaceans they love to eat along their native shorelines throughout northern South America. Both in the aviary, and in the wild, you will rarely find a Scarlet Ibis alone. The national bird of Trinidad and Tobago, this species typically gathers in large flocks, akin to a packed and bustling Queer dance club, preferring to stick together with others for safety, comfort, and revelry. Living up to twenty years, they remain dedicated to their community, demonstrating cooperative behaviors to support one other.

It is worth taking note of the deep commitment to community exhibited by the Scarlet Ibis. As a Queer person, you are a part of a minority identity group. Depending on other intersecting aspects of your identity, you might collectively feel marginalized and alone sometimes, especially in certain settings or groups of people. You will need a strong support network to mitigate feelings of isolation—folks who can provide solace, understanding, and affirmation. Although the colors of each Scarlet Ibis are boldly independent, they stick close to their network of support and, in so doing, comprise a bright tapestry of color that is more visible and more vibrant than any one bird on its own. No matter how independent you might be, be sure to cultivate your flock network—that special conglomeration of people connected by shared experience. These "birds of a feather" will bring much comfort and joy along your journey.

Stop Nine: Myna Joy

As you round your way towards the exit of the aviary, you will reach one of my favorite spots. Here, towards the back of the building, is where you will find the densest "forest" of the facility, with thick multi-story vegetation layers containing a host of species flittering about. You will be well-served to be patient and watch carefully in this area. In particular, you might be rewarded by two species of myna birds, part of a family of birds that includes the more familiar starlings. The two varieties, the Golden-Crested Myna* and Bali Myna,*** could not be more divergent in appearance. Both the size of an American Robin, the Golden-Crested is a glossy black bird with a bright yellow head and small yellow wing patches only visible when flying. The Bali Myna, on the other hand, is almost entirely snow-white in color, with black tips on the tail and wings and a blue eye patch of exposed skin. Both

hailing from the same geographic region of Southeast Asia (the Bali being confined only to a small area in Bali), these birds inhabit lowland forests and will often forage in the high canopy. Because they are usually so high in the trees, you might hear them before you see them. Like most birds in their family, along with a series of gurgles, croaks, and high-pitched notes like whistles, Mynas can mimic other sounds in their environment and can even replicate human voices, a trait that has unfortunately made them prized commodities in the underground pet trade.

Frankly, I've always wondered why these birds are so adept at mimicking other elements of their surroundings. Both stunning birds on their own, their skills at imitation seem unnecessary. They have little reason to be anything other than exactly what they are—gorgeous, highly intelligent, uniquely fashioned, ecologically important, and just plain fun creatures! In fact, the word "myna" is derived from two Sanskrit words that together are interpreted as "bubbling with joy," not altogether dissimilar from the "light-hearted and carefree" variation of the word "gay." If you watch these birds for long, you will see the characteristic jubilant bubble they exude—a joy that should be celebrated, not covered up with the replicated sounds and voices of others. As a Queer person, however you might define that aspect of your identity, every element of your one-of-a-kind being should also be celebrated. It is tempting to mimic the behaviors, opinions, and appearances of those in the majority. In fact, many of us are rather good at doing so, a strategy we learned early on as a way to hide our true selves. But your diversity adds vibrancy and purpose to the dense forest of humanity. Conformity is boring. You are an essential component of the rich tapestry of life—every single part of you.

Stop Ten: Exit & Pause

As much as you will hate to leave, you eventually must depart from this tropical oasis. Soon after you exit the building, you might take an opportunity to pause once more to relish the delight from which you have emerged. Constructed of geometric glass pieces fashioned into an almost complete dome structure, the architecture of the aviary is mesmerizing.

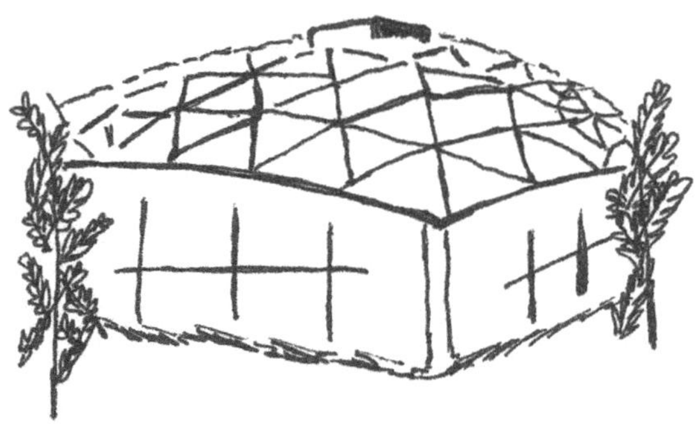

Reflect for a moment on the joyfully abundant tropical microcosm you just encountered. Did it come from pure fantasy? Was it all make-believe? Can it be real?

Especially as a Queer person, you might wish to stop and celebrate this safe space of wonder, a phenomenon not always easy to come by. From time to time, you might need to escape into places similar to this one. You might want to daydream, imagine, and travel far away from the harsh realities of the outside world. Let the aviary remind you to invest in finding and cultivating spaces just like this—places of blissful retreat when bitterness and anguish surrounds. Hold tight to the places where you feel beautiful, connected, whole, integrated, and loved—and value the people you find there. They will grant you grace throughout your life.

Departure Notes

With that, dear reader, your expedition through the aviary is complete. I hope your brief jaunt among our winged companions has revealed opportunities to take pride in your original plume, fly beyond the confines of those who wish to cage you, elevate your voice above the canopy's fray, behold the beauty of your identity, find dedicated and tender partners, flock towards deep, meaningful community, and—perhaps above all—to embrace the joy that you deserve. Although there is no place quite like the North Carolina Zoo aviary, you do not have to find yourself enclosed within a human-made tropical dome to experience the manna offered by our wild counterparts. May such magical encounters provide a rich rainbow of sustenance during your adventures through life.

Postscript

On April 21, 2022, the North Carolina Zoo announced that it was permanently closing the aviary habitat due to deferred maintenance and infrastructure deemed beyond repair. Among the many expansion and fundraising needs of the organization, birds no longer rise to the top. What was once a prized, heralded, unique attraction slowly fell out of favor among the new charismatic species and flashy revenue-generating enterprises at the zoo. The nearly 100 birds and hundreds of plants in the building have now been re-homed at other institutions or relocated to other areas of the zoo. The doors have been shuttered. Bird by bird and plant by plant, the place of magic and wonder of my childhood has been disassembled and closed. The closure represents a crushing loss of something treasured—a feeling not altogether dissimilar from the dejection experienced by Queer communities around the globe (including in the United States) where tenuous rights and protections are challenged, questioned, and sometimes even revoked.

Although the physical space that once was the aviary no longer exists, and while it is tempting to believe that the beauty it harbored has been permanently erased, I still visit that cherished place in my mind. I hear the hum of the air circulation system and the chirps, calls, and squawks of the residents; I smell the moist soil; and the many shades of green foliage flash across my field of vision as I walk that sacred interior path etched in my memory. Despite the sadness and grief that I feel about the death of such a place, I hold tight to the lessons I gathered beneath the tropical forest canopy it contained, a medicine for the soul that lives forever. The animals there were my sojourners and my friends. Because they delighted me through decades of questions and uncertainty, I owe them much.

I refuse to let that die.

Conversion Camp

A. Scott Henderson

It wasn't an actual camp. Everybody knew that. It was just something to be endured. But it'd be over tomorrow.

"We want to heal you," Brother John had told them when they first arrived. What a fuckin' joke, James thought.

James's parents felt differently. After he'd come out to them, their prayers had been judgmental and accusatory: "Lord, give James the strength to overcome his unnatural urges—to reject his sin and perversion." There was also an ultimatum. He either agreed to attend a conversion camp or there'd be no more money for college. The value of his soul was measured by the cost of his tuition.

So, off he went to Camp Grace. It was located in that righteous arc stretching from the lower South to the upper Midwest, a crescent of born-again backwaters. Every two weeks, a new group of thirty young men would sit in a circle listening to parables about ancient patriarchs disowning errant sons, dogma spewed in summer heat.

"How'd they find out about *you*?" James asked his roommate, both of them struggling to fall asleep on their first night in the sweltering dormitory.

Daniel, a college sophomore, hesitated. His linebacker body was uncomfortably shoehorned into a single bed. "Coach saw one of my texts. There was also a photo. He said I'd be cut from the team unless I got help."

"What a bunch of shit. I wonder how they'll know if we've been *helped*," James said, sarcasm dripping like the sweat from their bodies.

Now, two weeks later, a ceiling fan in the fellowship hall circulated the fetid air of damnation, paint peeling from perspiration. They spent the morning reviewing stuff they'd already covered, reminders of how *real* men were expected to talk, walk, and eat, what they were supposed to wear, which subjects to avoid.

It was a total waste of time. They'd learned these he-man lessons years ago. After all, that had been the entire point of the humiliating slurs and merciless fists they'd experienced on school playgrounds. Predictably, Brother John—with his Calvinist self-regard—believed that such bullying served a purpose. Didn't the Bible say, *The Lord strikes the wicked man in open sight of others*? Tomorrow couldn't come soon enough for James.

Most of the guys loitered outside after lunch. A few grabbed a quick smoke, the stink of sulfur replaced by unrepentant ashes. Others talked about getting their phones back—Brother John had confiscated them on the first day, sternly commanding, "Thou shalt not worship false gods."

A medium-sized dog threaded his way through the knots of conversation until he found James, who gave him a piece of desiccated cornbread. "See, I didn't forget you."

The dog had appeared on the second day of camp, an outcast roaming the parched landscape. Associating his black coat with the mythical hound that patrolled Hades, the guys had named him Cerberus. He and James had bonded almost immediately.

The afternoon session began by singing the camp's unofficial anthem, its testosterone laden lyrics—*Soldiers of our God arise, forward march with blood and fire*—were more akin to a violent computer game than a hymn. Which was exactly why James always refused to sing it.

Discussion of a verse from the Book of James came next: *Each person is tempted when they are dragged away by their own evil desire*. The guy sitting next to James whispered, "Dude, I didn't know you wrote that."

James stifled a laugh. "We were definitely dragged *here*," he responded under his breath. "Not that it's changed me one damn bit."

The day's final activity was role-playing. Grouped in pairs, the guys were given a detailed script on how to counsel a fictitious friend who had "relapsed." Like the Good Shepherd watching over his flock, Brother Luke—the camp's assistant director—made sure the guys didn't stray from the dialogue's exact wording.

Luke—he'd insisted there was no need to call him *Brother* Luke—was fresh out of divinity school. His shoulder-length hair, jeans, t-shirts, and swaggering two-day stubble made him the cool one, a youthful contrast to Brother John's crew-cut authoritarianism. Luke had asked James several times to play foosball with him in the dormitory's stygian basement. These overtures had made James wary. Did Luke sense his loathing of the camp—his determination to reject the castor oil of conversion?

Having completed their role-playing exercise (all the relapsed friends had been sternly rebuked), the guys were given free time before supper—their *Last* Supper, one of them acidly punned. James claimed a shaded bench and began throwing an old tennis ball for Cerberus.

Luke greeted him. "Hey," he said. He was shirtless, his hair tied in back. "Mind if I share your spot? Thought I'd take a short run." Luke squeezed onto the bench, his leg pressing against James, bare skin flirting with bare skin. James concentrated on throwing the ball.

Luke appeared in no hurry to re-lace his shoes. "I've really enjoyed getting to know you," he said. "You've probably noticed that I'm very attracted to you. In every way." As if to make that clear, he leaned over and kissed James, prickly lips pricking peach-fuzzed innocence. James pushed Luke away and stood up.

Luke didn't seem fazed. "I thought this was how you might react," he said. "I'm sorry. I truly am." He jogged off, the sound of his reproachful footfalls fading in the late-afternoon heat.

James was restless that night, his sleep interrupted by formless dread.

No wonder he was on edge when he met with Brother John the next morning, a final act of obedience that each camper had to perform prior to leaving.

"Brother Luke told me what happened yesterday," Brother John said. "I'm very disappointed." The words *Sinned, Saved, Sent Home* were printed on his shirt. "A normal young man would not have responded as you did," he added, hands folded on his desk, a patriarch and the errant son.

James's face became hot. He realized that yesterday had been a test.

Brother John sat as rigid as a church pew, right-angled and unsmiling. "You didn't need to return Luke's affection," he said, "but if you'd been making *any* effort to change, you wouldn't have been so...revolted...by his kiss."

James's hands were shaking under the table. He would *not* cry in front of Brother John.

"How many times do I have to say it," James pleaded hoarsely. "I have always been attracted to the *opposite* sex. I was born that way." His throat tightened. "I want to marry a *woman* one day—and if we have children, it *won't* be through artificial insemination or a surrogate."

Brother John looked away in disgust. "I spoke to your fathers on the phone this morning. Since you still have this abnormal—this *sinful*—attraction to women, they think you should stay for another two-week session. They said they'll be keeping you in their prayers."

His tears didn't start until he was back on the bench where Luke had kissed him. He watched the other guys, including Daniel, fist-bumping their farewells. Cerberus appeared out of the midday dust and lay beneath the bench.

James wiped the tears from his face. "It's only you and me, Cerb," he said. The dog's ears twitched. "But you can be damn sure we're gonna be outta here in two weeks." James began chewing a blade of dried-up grass.

"Here's the plan," he said. "Luke and I are gonna become friends. In fact, very *close* friends. I'll do anything—*anything* that's necessary to convince him that I've changed, that I've got the same desires he does."

James squinted off into the distance. "And I'll prove it to him as many times as he wants."

The air was dead still.

"Ya see, Cerb, I've got it all worked out. I'll just be role-playing—role-playing the whole fuckin' time. Because when you and I leave here, nobody's gonna doubt for one second that I'm a 100% red-blooded convert."

James walked slowly back to the dormitory, Cerberus close behind. It was already blistering. Hellish, actually.

By the Numbers

A. Scott Henderson

From: Batch.com
To: Scott Henderson

Thank you for purchasing a year's membership in Batch.com, the nation's largest online dating service! To get you off to a great start, we have used U.S. Census data to gather information about your local community:

U.S. Census data for Greenville County, South Carolina:

547,827	Total population
397,106	Adults (men and women 18+ years old)
192,596	Adult men
43,117	Adult men in your age cohort
13,797	Adult single men in your age cohort
1,828	Adult single men in your age and education cohort
37*	Adult single gay men (estimated) in your age and education cohort

**Information about employment, relationship goals, political beliefs, tobacco use, health/fitness, and substance abuse is unknown. Individuals might or might not be Batch.com members.*

P.S. If your preferences were *heterosexual women* instead of *gay men*, then your potential dating pool would increase from 37 to 2,446. Please let us know if you would like for us to make that change in your Batch.com profile. Your happiness is our only goal!

Dating the Dead

A. Scott Henderson

From: LGBTQ Dating Professionals
To: Scott Henderson

Good news! We've found a possible match for you. Barry is a college English professor in Pulaski, Tennessee, which is just around the corner from Greenville. He is highly educated, shares your political/social views, exercises regularly, enjoys similar hobbies/interests, has a sense of humor, and is drug/disease free. He is the same age as you and eager for a serious relationship. We think the two of you would really hit it off! Let us know if you would like to proceed with this match.

From: LGBTQ Dating Professionals
To: Scott Henderson

We're delighted that you've approved the match with Barry! We'll email you his phone number, after which it will be up to you to contact him.

P.S. In regard to your comment about the Appalachian Mountains, we're aware that their location—combined with snow, ice, rain, flooding, and/or rockslides—will probably extend the six-hour driving time between you and Barry. Still, we'd like to think that nothing can get in the way of true love...LOL!

From: LGBTQ Dating Professionals
To: Scott Henderson

We apologize for not sending you Barry's phone number. Sadly, we haven't been able to reach him. Please consider the match cancelled, effective immediately. We'll let you know if Barry resurfaces. In the meantime, we'll continue to search for your ideal match. Patience is the key to success!

From: LGBTQ Dating Professionals
To: Scott Henderson

Thanks for offering to assist us in contacting Barry. However, to repeat our message of earlier today, we've already canceled the match. You also inquired about whether this cancellation might be "a bit premature." As the nation's largest personalized LGBTQ matchmaking service, we've had a great deal of experience in such things. You're in excellent hands with us!

From: LGBTQ Dating Professionals
To: Scott Henderson

We're disappointed that you think something sounds "fishy" because we canceled the match with Barry "so quickly." Our least satisfied members are those who've decided—for some silly reason or another—that they can't trust us. We're convinced you're not one of those people!

⁂

From: LGBTQ Dating Professionals
To: Scott Henderson

You clearly violated our dating rules by trying to find Barry after we had canceled the match. Nonetheless, we can confirm that the information you found about him on the internet is accurate.

To answer your question, no—we didn't realize he was dead. (Thank you for including a copy of his obituary—that's a very good photo of him!) As we're sure you'll understand, our large number of clients makes it impossible for us to update our records more often than every few years. We eventually reached Barry's mother, who told us of his death. She was apparently unaware of his membership in LGBTQ Dating Professionals (or, as she put it, "in that kind of group").

We must again emphasize that you shouldn't have pursued the match after we told you not to do so. This situation could've been avoided if you'd followed *all* of the 108 rules in our "Don't Do It Dating Guidelines," which we've attached as a friendly reminder.

⁂

From: LGBTQ Dating Professionals
To: Scott Henderson

We strongly object to your use of the word "lying." We were *not* lying about Barry's "condition" when we said that we would notify you if he "resurfaced." We simply meant that we'd contact you if we found someone *similar* to him.

P.S. We believe you should focus more on the future and less on the past. Negativity always proves to be the kiss of death. Just a word to the wise!

From: LGBTQ Dating Professionals
To: Scott Henderson

There was no reason for sarcasm in your last email (i.e., your comment about "graverobbers"). We're trying to be as helpful as possible. In that vein, you should be pleased to know that we're going to make you a Priority Member at no extra charge (a $2,500 savings!). This means you'll never need to worry about being matched with someone who's no longer active.

From: LGBTQ Dating Professionals
To: Scott Henderson

We're sorry you think being upgraded to a Priority Member is simply our way of making sure that proposed matches "aren't listed on death certificates" (we prefer the phrase "no longer available"). As for your remark about the Better Business Bureau, we're no longer affiliated with them due to disagreements over complaints that were mistakenly filed against us. (We seem to attract people whose only desire is to smear our reputation.) Our advice is to keep moving forward. Your next match will probably be identified in no time!

From: LGBTQ Dating Professionals
To: Scott Henderson

Regrettably, we cannot grant your request to refund your money. The contract you signed specified that the membership fee was non-refundable (see Appendix 3, Section 5, Subsection 2, Part B, Exception 4, line 7). This allows us to spend more time finding matches for you instead of getting bogged down in legal technicalities.

From: LGBTQ Dating Professionals
To: Scott Henderson

We were shocked to learn that you think the $4,500 you paid to join LGBTQ Dating Professionals was the "worst decision" you've ever made. Though we haven't been able to provide you with any matches *yet* (not counting Barry), it's only been a handful of years since you became a member. Think of that $4,500 as an investment in your happiness, an investment that will pay huge dividends once you've found your soulmate. Isn't that a better way of looking at things? We think so!

P.S. In response to your question, the contract you signed does *not* indicate a date by which we need to have provided you with a certain number of matches. Fortunately, this means we don't have to worry about any artificial deadlines that might force us to offer you unsatisfactory matches.

⁂

From: LGBTQ Dating Professionals
To: Scott Henderson

We can't agree with you that our lack of deadlines makes us "unaccountable." Our tireless matchmakers work a minimum of eight (sometimes even ten) hours a week on behalf of our members. More to the point, deadlines would reduce us to nothing more than a business. While LGBTQ Dating Professionals has been accused of many things, nobody has ever claimed that we're half-hearted in recruiting new members. We're proud to serve people who are tired of being scammed by online dating services.

⁂

From: LGBTQ Dating Professionals
To: Scott Henderson

Has it really been two years since you last heard from us? How time flies!

A big YES to your question about whether we're still trying to find a match for you. Cupid never sleeps...LOL! However, we couldn't disagree more when you say that your age is "a distinct liability among gay men." Admittedly, since you joined LGBTQ Dating Professionals four years ago, you and Barry (he also thought outside the box!) have been the only members in your age group who haven't wanted to date younger men, i.e., men who are *decades* younger. But younger men don't have it easy either. Even though we usually find matches for our 18- to 25-year-old members in a couple of hours, for others in that age range it can sometimes take a few days or even a whole week—imagine how *they* must feel.

We encourage you to remain optimistic about your prospects. Someone is bound to find your age appealing!

❦

From: LGBTQ Dating Professionals
To: Scott Henderson

Oops! Thanks for pointing out our mistake. You have indeed been a member of LGBTQ Dating Professionals for eight, not four years. Nevertheless, we have a feeling that nine is going to be your lucky number!

Imposter Syndrome

Riley Hughes

Originally written to be performed as a spoken word poem.

What do you see when you look at me?
An absence of stereotypes that have been defined
by society?
A false identity?

My truth is synonymous with imposter
simultaneously wanting to be seen, affirmed,
but don't want to foster
the hateful labels given to me.

Why then do I feel confused?
Lacking a muse
to find my truth
I want to be accepted, but by whom?

I look straight
I'm not gay-enough
I go every day wondering
am I fake?!

To be Queer
to be in fear
worried whether my identity will appear.

Too hetero passing for LGBT,
too LGBT for those who know me.
Where then
do I fit in the community?

But what do I know?
On the surface
there is no rainbow
just me, loving who I love
based on heart alone.

How do I beat this imposter syndrome?
Felt by many, not just some
because all I want
is to exist in peace
and resist the urge of society
to succumb
to the pressure
to change my identity
based on the perception of me.

Caryatids

Kevin Kao

Terracotta, 2018
(dimensions vary)

Much of my work can be viewed through the lens of cultural hybridity: drawing from personal narrative, body, and multiplicity as avenues of assimilation. Much like the Ancient Greek Caryatid porch adorning the Erechtheion (Temple of Athena) on the Acropolis, this work, *Caryatids*, positions the figure as a conjecture of structure, space, and the socially constructed body. Though seemingly gender-less, each bust is coded through the inferences of hair: biomorphic, suggestive, and fluid. Similarly, the ideal is replaced with an alternative—the Other in multiplicity.

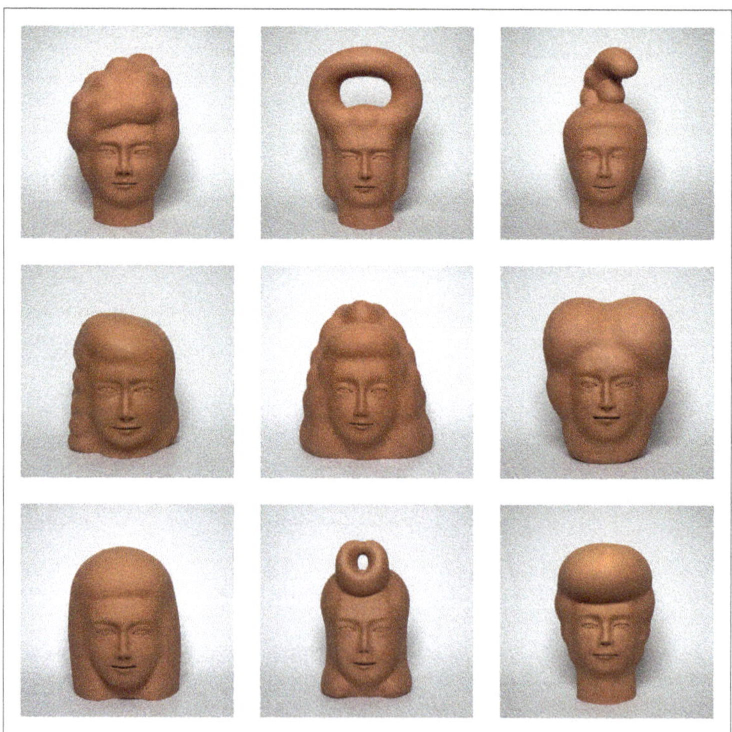

Hubris (Rome)

Kevin Kao

Ceramic and glaze, 2019
24" x 15" x 6"

Drawn from a series exploring hubris as funny failure through reflection and gaze, *Hubris (Rome)* imagines the myth of Rome's foundation as a paired portrait and mirror. Akin to Narcissus peering into the void, this piece places Queerness as reflection of self both figuratively and literally.

Gay 101

Nicholas Radel

I came out in the early 1970s, never really feeling the kind of bias that's the stuff of literary legend, even in ultra-conservative Cincinnati. It existed, but it wouldn't come for me until later, as an adult, after I moved South to teach. Surprisingly enough, even my high school was "enlightened," if you understand that to mean that one of my friends had another friend who was openly gay, and by my senior year had made it clear that "if I was like Jack" it was okay with her. I didn't corroborate her perceptive glance, but in her Midwestern way, she confirmed her good will abounding.

The times were primed for sexual subterfuge, and I didn't live the life some tolerant people today seem to want for young gay, lesbian, and transgender people. I wasn't in mourning because I'd never be normal, whatever that means. I was thrilled not to be. I wasn't ashamed, and at least in my public life, I didn't hide my feelings or moderate my eccentricities. I didn't believe heterosexuals were a superior class of people—and delighted, really, in puncturing their sometimes over-inflated image of themselves. I could be plenty tragic about love (I lamented that the silken-skinned, blue-eyed David Cage would only ever be my platonic friend), but I wasn't tragic about being Queer, ever.

Being gay (as I was before we had the term "Queer") was a welcome displacement from the ordinary that, I hope, at least some young Queer people feel today. It was a force field against social conformity, a platform to shout the shocking, and a space in which to absorb the new. Being gay was the most important spur to my self-knowledge. I was educated in a very fine college preparatory school in Cincinnati, and it provided me important opportunities for self-scrutiny and tools for careful social analysis. But learning to be gay was the key that opened the wider world for me. My sexuality is primary; it is one of my native languages.

A DEFINING MOMENT OF MY GAY YOUTH came when I met a jolly band of resisting drag queens and gay men. Lauren, Christy, Bobby, and Jake were a small part of Cincinnati's homegrown "Gay Liberation Front." I walked up the dark stairwell to their apartment, in one of those Cincinnati buildings that have two entrance doors on the left, one to the downstairs apartment and another opening directly onto the stairs leading up. "Find Hope All Who Enter Here," a sign on the door should have said. My first impression was vivid—Lauren DeMichaels twirling with a fez-like hive of hair, a dervish in a yellow duster. She was seeking advice from Christy, Cincinnati's drag mistress of the "duster number." How could she make her cape spiral flat at the top so that her exquisitely made-up face and stacked hair would seem to float on golden angels' wings? Christy was an inspiring goddess and her advice on drag couture was highly esteemed. On gay matters, her word was absolute. She lived with Bobby, a striking man whose size made him literally statuesque in drag, and Jake (more about him later).

Christy and Bobby had recently been arrested for soliciting on West Fourth Street. Before it became a fashionable haunt of the emerging Yuppie class, the street was a cruising ground for men who had not found a trick at the nearby disco, Badlands.

Always unflappable, Christy matter-of-factly described her arrest. Settling between the legs of a mustachioed clone in his hotel room, she glanced up to see him holding his police badge like a defensive shield, at crotch level.

"You're under arrest."

"Oh well," she replied, "I guess I'd better put my heels back on then."

The girls were brave. They challenged their arrests in court when Ohio was revising its criminal code and repealing its laws on sodomy and solicitation. They shantayed away free women.

All four helped ease me out of the closet. In Cincinnati, we called it "bringing someone out," as if it was a formal educational service for the young and benighted, and of course it was. Lauren DeMichaels ushered me out into the Queer arena. Not because I found her especially attractive in or out of drag; rather, I had decided that, at seventeen, it was time to stop making such a big deal of "coming out." So, I vowed to do it with the next man who asked. And Tommy (Lauren undressed) asked. It was a sunny Saturday afternoon at a gay picnic organized by the fledgling University of Cincinnati gay group. Tommy invited me, with one eyebrow raised, for a walk through Mt. Storm Park. Conveniently, we discovered a wall of bushes bent over an enclosed space—a natural bower of bliss into which my gay Acrasia tempted me. With his tight cut-offs, tan legs, and slim hips, Tommy was right enough for the moment.

But when, a week later, I ended up alone in his apartment after my best friend abandoned me, I found myself where I really didn't want to be—in his arms again, this time on a bed.

Today, some might see Tommy as predatory. The homosexual as vampire-like seducer still turns up in gay popular works—the 2018 film version of Gerrard Conley's *Boy Erased* or Fred Hersch's 2017 memoir *Good Things Happen Slowly*. In both, the predator takes advantage of our young hero, revealing his depraved and threatening homosexual self over and against the hero's more noble one. But Tommy was, as we all always are, feeling his way into his then-present Queerness. He said, earnestly, he was doing me a favor, teaching me to give as well as receive. I'm laughing at his utter seriousness as I write this (just as I did afterward back then). If the lesson was slightly distasteful, perhaps too advanced for my skill level, it wasn't entirely Tommy's fault. He was an unimaginative romantic who thought of me as a catch worth reeling in. But he was also, after all, the means to my end. I was getting the coming-out thing out of the way, and I got Tommy out of the way shortly thereafter.

Christy made a play, and because she was a charming hostess, I felt I shouldn't say no. And then Bobby did, too. But having been acquainted already with both Lauren's and Christy's prickly, freshly-shaved, naked chests, I declined politely. So, when sweet, hairy-chested Jake, an older man of twenty-one, intimated that I might share his bed, I took him up on the offer. As seventeen-year-olds do, I developed a little crush on him. He was so kind. So unassuming. And when I decided I could make my own way in the world, he helped ease that transition, too.

My mother didn't know I was gay, and being a single parent, she worried. She knew I had gay friends, and she usually pitied them for what she saw as the inevitable family dysfunction that produced them.

"That poor David Cage," she said one day after he had hung our phone receiver upside-down in the kitchen (his resistance to the normal).

"Do you think he's gay because his mother ran off and left him?"

"It's a theory," I replied.

I used my friendship with David as an excuse for getting out of the house and into Jake's bed. And my mother—hilariously—would deflect her worries about my homosexuality onto the perils of drinking and driving.

"Did David drink?," she asked.

"No!" I didn't lie—he "smoked."

"Did he drink and drive?"

"Certainly not." Again, I didn't lie.

"Well, homosexuals have problems with alcohol," she pronounced, "and I don't want you to be out in cars with drunken homosexuals."

Such expressions of practical wisdom made her a favorite with my friends. And for years, I issued stern warnings to my gay companions who held the car keys at parties. But I was honest in assuring my mother that I would not be "out in cars with drunken homosexuals." What I didn't say is that I'd be in bed with one, drunken or otherwise.

Christy, Bobby, Jake, and Lauren felt that under their tutelage I had become a "well-adjusted homosexual," and they all beamed at me with pride. Never had they met someone my age who came out with so little trauma. They were right, and they had helped me immeasurably. But I was worried. Was I becoming a slut? My other friends wondered, too, if I were not perhaps being, as they put it, "easy easy." Easy was one thing, but *easy easy*? Enough said in Catholic Cincinnati.

I decided to cool it for a while. I'd learned my lessons about coming out, and there was no need for additional training. In the late fall of my senior year in high school, I decided—virtuously—that I would not have sex again until I met someone with whom I could be "serious." And for better or worse, in August after graduation, I met another older man, a twenty-two-year-old.

Reader, I fell in love with him and, for the next six years, he taught me everything he knew.

But I was already the wiser.

What You Never Know

Nicholas Radel

It was as tawdry as it could be, little more than a backyard tent for a dull lawn party. I—we—had imagined the silk draperies of a Bedouin prince on a windy escarpment, with half-nude boys tending to one's comfort inside. In those days, the backrooms and tented areas of gay bars where men went to have sex were things of the big city; our image of the "Orgy Temple" was straight out of movies for bored housewives. In the Midwest, we still thought about romance and kissing. We had no idea about the gay sex-scapes emerging in New York, San Francisco, and the City of Angels.

But the Orgy Temple was dark enough to be private, and I didn't know if Geoff was there.

"Geoff," I whispered.

"Leave me alone." I could barely make him out as he stepped over the slurping and humping bodies, squeezing under the back flap of the tent and knocking down a support pole as he left.

"God damn it," someone shouted, giving his jaws a rest as he fixed the pole.

It was, I guessed, the end of my first delirious summer romance, so I stopped chasing Geoff, and took my misery elsewhere, behind the speakers near the dance floor where Claudja Barry was singing about her "Boogie, Oogie, Boogie, Woogie Dancin' Shoes."

Today, if you ask someone about a city in Indiana, they will inevitably name Indianapolis, a town that has much improved in past years. But in the 1970s we called it Indy-A-No-Place. The real capital of Indiana, the social and cultural center, was Bloomington. And, in its own way, it was a gay capital, thanks in part to the pioneering sex researcher Dr. Alfred Kinsey and his great supporter Herman B. Wells, the president of the university. They made the campus and the town safe for people of all stripes, even gay and lesbian ones. Little Bloomington had gay bars, dance halls, dirty bookstores, and weekly Integrity meetings at the home of the local, gay Episcopalian minister, Father Taylor, whose presence promised grace even before death and resurrection. On the street there was a free and easy flow of gay life.

I wasted my first year in that paradise. I cleaned sick folks' dishes at the hospital, and the 5:30 morning shift made it feel a little like I had left Oz rather than found it. Besides, I was in a six-year relationship with Eddie back in Cincinnati, and my divided attention meant I failed to grasp the wonders in front of me. Prig that I was, I remained faithful two full years. But by the time my second summer rolled around, things changed. Eddie had lost interest, and so had I. I was ready to meet a boy like Geoff. And one June night in 1979, I watched the sun come up over Lake Monroe, with him in my arms.

I'd seen Geoff around (you couldn't miss his blue eyes). An art major, he idolized Milton Glaser, the celebrated graphic designer. He was the first (but not the last) gay man I've met who expressed his love of beauty through his face. He spent hours designing it, as if it were a poster announcing his coming. Once, I tried to pull him away from his mirror.

"Please, let's go dancing NOW." And he replied, wisely enough, that the world was so ugly the least he could do was try to look as good as possible facing it.

I met him formally through my friend Luke, another Bloomington A-lister I had no hope of bedding. Swarthy, dark, and thin with a heavy mustache, Luke had once had a cigarette slapped from his lips by the temperamental actress Cloris Leachman, who was in Vevay, Indiana, filming *A Girl Named Sooner*. Luke was a gopher on the set who dared smoke in the great one's presence. That slap knocked his Marlboro ten feet away—and gave Luke a cultural cachet that only added to his great beauty, neither of which would survive the coming epidemic.

Luke seemed to love Geoff for a while. Both were Indiana boys: Geoff a pampered, middle-class suburban kid from South Bend who felt at home in sophisticated Chicagoland; and Luke, a solid small-town Midwesterner not fond of drama unless delivered as resoundingly as Leachman's slap. But one night, for no apparent reason, he ditched Geoff at the Gentry Remedy Company.

I felt sorry for Geoff. It wasn't hard to understand what it would be like to lose Luke—if, that is, you could imagine having had him in the first place. Geoff's wasn't the only heart he had broken, so I identified with Geoff more than anything else. For his part, Geoff clung to me for answers about my friend I really didn't have. What had happened? Why did Luke leave? Did I think he'd come back? Back then (maybe it's safe to say it forty years later), every failed relationship—especially a significant one—could be proof that a gay boy didn't deserve to be loved. It made him fear he would never find love again.

But my motives weren't pure. So hungry was I to be in Geoff's presence, so thrilled to have made a connection with him, that I gave him my absolute attention. When the moment was right, I suggested we leave the disco to talk about Luke some more, to analyze his motives and ascertain his next moves—anything to keep those blue eyes trained on me. I had no hope Geoff would ever be in my bed. To the contrary, the certainty that I was not in his league gave me courage to do everything I could to stay with him the rest of the night.

When we couldn't drink one more cup of awful Waffle House coffee, with its miserable non-dairy creamer, I suggested we drive the thirty or so miles to Lake Monroe. And because it was chilly as we sat talking in the life-guard's chair, I thought nothing of Geoff's sliding ever closer to me, until he asked, "can I kiss you?"

In that moment, Eddie was history. And though Luke was a friend, he made it clear the next night at work that Geoff was out of the picture for him. So, I called Geoff to re-arrange my life—first, dancing at the Gentry and then home to bed.

It was an especially hot summer. Bloomington is built on good Indiana limestone, and local myth has it that there are hot springs underneath. Since neither one of us was taking summer classes, we didn't really have to get out of bed until it was time to work or go dancing. I was studying for my first qualifying exam in drama, but when the choice was *The Play Called Corpus Christi* or sliding Geoff out of his pants, a sensible man chose carefully. A sensible man also nearly flunked his exam. But the summer wore on in a discernible pattern. Geoff and I typically lived three weeks in bliss, followed by one week of trauma.

Because of Geoff, I met the "important" people in town—those gay men who knew all the beautiful people. I was a tag-along to beauty. Others must have thought so, too, because one night one of my friends remarked that I was becoming an A-lister myself—not for my looks, he added too quickly, but my personality. I guess so. I had become known, someone to invite. Geoff's partner. I was gay respectable, a fledgling idea at the time, but one that would lead years later to gay marriage! How could I have known? Because he was of a certain class, Geoff had friends in fraternities; at least once a week we went dancing at the local "straight" disco, Ye Olde Regulator. And we ate in marginally classier places, which put a strain on my budget, leading to extra shifts waiting tables and a longing for the fall crowds at football season.

But if respectability was new, and thus an inviting sensation, it was not the glimpses of gay life outside the ghetto that drew me to Geoff. It was his velvet skin, auburn hair, and blue eyes—and his skill as a lover. Hail, unwedded love! Chicagoland had obviously taught him more than Cincinnati ever knew. But, true to form, we found ourselves coming apart again at the start of week twelve. It was a Friday night, and Geoff lay on top of me in bed and began to cry. When I asked him what was wrong, he raised his head from my chest, looked soulfully into my eyes, and blurted out, "I think I'm madly in love with you!"

I laughed.

I had just come off a six-year relationship. So, I foolishly thought I knew something about love. Surely it took more than six weeks. I hadn't yet learned that most essential lesson: in love and sex, reality rarely matters; illusion is everything. I should have said that's just how I felt, too, that I laughed because I was so happy to hear my feelings reciprocated. I should have seized the moment, kissed him deliriously from head to toe, taking him molecule by molecule into my very heart of hearts. But, like Luke, I was a practical Midwesterner, and so I tried hard to make distinctions: "Very fond," I said; "I love you, but I'm not in love. It takes time."

"YOU NINCOMPOOP!" MY FRIEND RIMA SHRIEKED into the phone. "You said what? You've really lost him now."

And given that Geoff was inconsolable—he had demanded that I leave his bed and house immediately—I really thought I had. What followed was a week of sly attempts to insinuate myself back into his arms. Counseling from Rima. Calls unanswered. Then tearful answerings, stymied by Geoff's unstoppable fury. He had convinced himself that I deliberately roused him from slumber on my chest to say I didn't love him, which in his mind also meant I couldn't love him.

What saved us, briefly, was the Orgy Temple.

⁂

As I've said, my social prospects had improved with Geoff. And during the course of our much-watched love affair, which we delighted in playing out in public, we were invited to the premier gay event of the Bloomington season—the huge party hosted yearly by the owners of the town's most successful spa and boutique, held in an old farmhouse on acres of land outside town. It was Bloomington's answer to Fire Island, I suppose. In our naive circle, it had the mystique of the Circuit. Everyone gay who was anyone gay was invited, and that summer so were Geoff and I.

It was imperative that we patch things up.

In the several weeks before my disastrous laugh, Geoff and I had really focused on this White Party in the sticks, building it up in our minds. We would arrive at our destination, a mansion on a large estate, a long driveway stretching lazily to the house. We'd be greeted with Champagne and enter a sophisticated adult world of desire. What really sparked our imagination was the rumor that our hosts provided a large tent to facilitate whatever romantic rendezvous might develop in the languorous night—the Orgy Temple. Neither Geoff nor I intended to indulge. We were young Midwesterners, after all. A kiss, a blow, those practices reserved for special occasions—and true romance—were more our speed. But our curiosity was aroused, and we were determined to check out the scene however briefly, just to be in the know.

We left town piled together, six in a small car. Geoff sat between my legs, and because I held him close, I could sense he was unsure of himself and of us. For the first time it occurred to me that his reaction wasn't simply gay drama, but deeply felt hurt.

Schooled by Rima, I figured I would use the party to make amends: a stroll under the stars, a kiss, an apology, and a profession of love. And on such a night as that! Rural Indiana is exquisite at midnight in August. The stars shine in a wholly black sky, and the air chills for the first time that day. I was sure it would remind Geoff of our night on Lake Monroe.

When we arrived, I wasted no time leading him down a hill toward a distant field and a small, wooded area where I kissed him. It would have been very romantic if it hadn't been for two boys fucking, who came into view within spitting distance as our eyes adjusted to the darkness. But I gracefully moved Geoff away, toward a quieter place, and kissed him again.

"I love you," I said, trying to sound convincing.

He drew back, looking confused. "No, you don't."

And then I did it again: "Well, maybe it's not really love ..."

Before I could finish, he was out of my arms, heading up the hill, stumbling over the fucking boys, and then out of sight.

He wouldn't talk to me after that. Where he went, I followed. Where I arrived, he left. In my dull way I had killed the party, at least for us, though we spent the night threading through it, from pool to dance floor to conversation rooms and, yes, the Orgy Temple.

Claudja was singing about her "Dancin' Shoes," and I tried to hide behind the speakers that blared her voice. One boy, Curtis, spied me out and tried to comfort me. He brought me a drink and the usual advice: "You can have any boy you want." But kindly Curtis only made things worse, for it wasn't "any boy" I wanted.

By some miracle Geoff and I ended up in the backseat of the same car for our ride home. He sat stiffly on my lap, exhausted. Halfway there he leaned his head on my chest and fell asleep, another blessing I couldn't have wished for or deserved. We slept together uneasily that night, and over the next few days tried to repair our broken love. But things weren't going to work out, and when classes started in September, we found an excuse to drift apart. We danced in the same bars, sometimes together. But we arrived alone and left separately. We were no longer an item. Neither of us dated again while we were both in Bloomington, which gave me muted hope.

Then, in October, Geoff dropped out of school to make his fortune in New York. He told me his decision one night when we met by accident on the dance floor. He teared up a little, then walked up the four or five steps to the exit, where he disappeared again into the night.

I SAW GEOFF ONCE MORE BY CHANCE, five years later in New York. There he was, suddenly, in a pharmacy at the corner of Christopher Street and Greenwich Avenue. He worried, typically, that he didn't look his best. I told him that he always looked good to me, which made him smile. And then we laughed. I gathered he had been successful, and that he was happy.

Afterwards, however, I had to conjure him from the dead to offer apologies. Recently, when I was in New York for a month, I regularly walked past his apartment on West 18th Street. I went there deliberately, longing to see him again. On some nights, he seemed as present to me as on that night he declared his love. Then one strange evening, I heard a window open and looked up to see him stick his head out.

"You can't tell a man he doesn't love you when he says he does."

"No," I replied, "that's not something you can do."

"Are you still in love with me?"

"Madly," I added, and blew him a kiss.

Small change for so much learning.

Honk For Jesus

Roger Sneed

Since the 2022 premiere of *Honk For Jesus. Save Your Soul* on the Peacock streaming service and its release in theaters, I have been fascinated by the responses popping up on Facebook and elsewhere about who or what the movie is really about. Some have said that it is *not* about the Black Church and a few have concentrated solely on Regina Hall's excellent performance, while still others have focused on the Black Church's oppression and suppression of Black women.

I am not writing this to overturn or contradict any of those views. A piece of art will always elicit multiple perspectives and possibly contradicting views. I want to specifically highlight the homoeroticism, phobias, and ambivalence at work in this movie.

Honk is clearly informed by the New Birth/Eddie Long scandal. Eddie Long was a Black minister who became pastor of the New Birth Missionary Baptist Church in 1987. Located in Cedartown, Georgia, the church's membership expanded greatly under Long's leadership. In 2010, four young men accused Long of sexual misconduct. They alleged that he plied them with all manner of gifts and money in exchange for sex. Once the allegations went public, many people left New Birth. Long, who died in 2017, steadfastly denied the allegations. While he was alive, Long was quite notably homophobic in his sermons. He was also quite notably hypermasculinist. He wore velour muscle shirts that were in vogue at the time, and virtually thumped his chest every other Sunday about masculinity.

When I lived in Atlanta in the late 1990s, I attended a party where one of the guests complained about Long's homophobia, arguing that Second Sunday—a discussion group for Black gay and bisexual men—should confront Long. I asked that person why he, a regular New Life attendee, could not seek an audience with him—after all, why would Eddie Long, then at the height of his popularity and fame—grant an audience to a group of openly gay Black men who didn't attend his church? More than a few Black gay men went to New Birth at that time who had to sit through Long's homophobic bloviations. I certainly remember hearing about them almost every month. Open and affirming Black churches for Black LGBT people were few and far between. The Black church scene in Atlanta revolved around the identity of the Black male preacher, the kind of preacher portrayed in *Honk*. And the identity of the Black male preacher was—and continues to be—a cross between pimp, prophet, and priest. He is expected to be attractive (or at least give off an aura of attractiveness), well-coiffed with impeccable sartorial choices, possess sermonic abilities that cause parishioners to "fall out" (i.e., become imbued with the Holy Spirit), and—above else—he has to be unflagging in his heterosexuality (or, at a minimum, to *appear* completely heterosexual).

This highlights the intersection of three enormous ongoing problems in the Black Church: homophobia/heterosexism, androcentrism, and classism/consumerism. I think that is where the movie's protagonist Lee-Curtis Childs (Sterling K. Brown) resides. He is either gay or bisexual, though the film seems to indicate that he's gay and very deeply closeted; the one sex scene with his wife Trinitie (Regina Hall) is a cringeworthy example of his engaging in an imitation of gay sex with her. He is obsessed with material goods and completely ignores Trinitie's own gifts, choosing to treat her as his accessory. He is so besotted with his position that he cannot reconcile his sexuality with himself or Trinitie, who clearly knows about his desires for young men. Further, Long is convinced that his status as a male guarantees him the right to be a pastor. His androcentrism is so overwhelming that he cannot fathom how far he has fallen by the movie's end. The classism/ consumerism that completes this triad is suffused throughout the movie and serves as a shield and cloak for both his and Trinitie's inner lives.

That Trinitie clearly knows that her husband has engaged in sexual encounters with other men is telling, as is her driving desire to "return" to some prior state of relative ignorance, all in service of maintaining the lifestyle to which she has become accustomed. Her own mother urges her to stay in the marriage. Echoing Savannah's mother (Starletta DuPois) in the 1995 film version of Terry McMillan's novel *Waiting To Exhale*, Trinitie's mother (Avis-Marie Barnes)—no doubt a recipient of Lee-Curtis's largesse—tells Trinitie that she doesn't sound like a Christian and that she should pray away her negative thoughts about her husband, furthering the movie's messages about the toxic effects that misogyny, homophobia, and rampant materialism have on the Black Church.

One thing I don't think the movie does well is to give the viewer a good sense of Lee-Curtis's inner life. We do not see him talking to any family members other than his wife—and his past lovers/victims want nothing to do with him. The closest peek we get at Lee-Curtis's interior world is the baptism scene, where his disrobing on stage symbolizes his dropping the mask. The expensive designer church clothes are in themselves a costume—a straitjacket that keeps him from being—or fully knowing—himself. The church's homophobia becomes *his* homophobia, as he steadfastly declares that he is "not a pervert." The clothes, the affluence, the conditional acceptance and "reverence" for his wife and his former church are what tells him he is not like "those people." This is the danger of the Black Church's homophobia, its misogyny, its classism—it *becomes* part of the people, distorting how they view themselves and others. The sin is that it warps the *imago dei* ("image of God") beyond sense and reason, leaving its victims to further warp other people's *imago dei*.

Black scholars of religion, theologians, and laypersons often talk of the Black Church as an institution. Such a description is useful when those of us in the academy attempt to make sense of the long history of the Black Church, its "being" in the lives of Black people, and how it has functioned as a refuge for them. However, such an approach can sometimes suggest that the Black Church is monolithic. That is not dissimilar from academic approaches to Black people(s). Black liberation and womanist theologies have attempted to situate themselves as the more "accurate" theology of the Black Church. Nevertheless, as those theologies have been informed (at least in part) by the Black Protestant Church, they have also been informed by the Black Protestant Church's homophobia. As such, they've not been fully capable of examining Black LGBT religious and spiritual lives. Quiet as kept, it's easier for Black theologians/scholars of religion to address *Honk*'s presentation of misogynoir than its presentation of homophobia. Furthermore, Black liberation and womanist theology as fields of intellectual inquiry do not often address Black popular culture and its intersection(s) with Black religious life. As I note in *The Dreamer and the Dream: Afrofuturism and Black Religious Thought* (Ohio State University Press, 2021), I suspect that that lack of engagement is due to a quest for relevance, as well as the prevailing view that analyses of popular culture are not "serious" scholarship.

On the other hand, reactions from Black laypersons to *Honk* have been mixed. Via social media such as Twitter and Facebook, some have taken issue with the unflattering picture of the Black Church that the movie paints. Twitter user "@CarltonJordan" noted that his mother and friends were upset by the movie; in a subsequent post, he shared a screenshot of a Facebook post in which a person described it as "degrading to predominantly Black churches." While this particular post did not mention Lee-Curtis's sexuality, it noted that not all Black preachers act as Lee-Curtis does in *Honk*.

In a version of this essay that I posted on Facebook, I wrote: "If the Black Church is to BE the church, it has to renounce misogyny, classism, and homophobia. If it is to be as prophetic as it claims to be, it must renounce the idolatry of the Black male preacher—an idolatry that has led to the *cult* of the Black preacher. Those within the Black Church have had—and are having—some tough-ass questions to ask. #honkforjesussaveyoursoul just started asking some of them."

I take issue with what I wrote then. Perhaps it is because I am, at best, generally ambivalent about the potential for the Black Church to be a prophetic institution. I have written a version of that statement for close to twenty years, ever since I began my graduate studies in religion. While *Honk* poses (albeit clumsily) some very good questions about the Black Church and sexuality, I am not convinced that it or any other well entrenched American institution is capable of being more than a vehicle for classism, elitism, and dated gender and sexual politics. Perhaps what *Honk* is subtly telling us is that the Black Church of yesteryear is gone, and that we must find other pastures, other homes, other safe and nurturing spaces.

MUNA Gets It

Brandon Tensley

I gush often about the indie band MUNA, a Queer pop sensation formed by Katie Gavin, Josette Maskin, and Naomi McPherson in 2013. With earwormy tracks such as "I Know a Place," "End of Desire," and "Pink Light," it's easy to see why the group is so beloved. But in addition to its general catchiness, the band also just gets it.

And by "it," I mean that the members of MUNA understand the power of embracing Queer desire—a notion that feels all the more revolutionary and urgent at a moment filled with reinvigorated threats against Queer people.

Take "What I Want," the final single from the band's self-titled third album, released during Pride Month in June 2022. "I want the full effects / I wanna hit it hard / I wanna dance in the middle of a gay bar," lead singer and songwriter Katie Gavin sings on the chorus. "I want the fireworks / I want the chemistry / I want that girl right over there to wanna date me."

I want, I want, I want. Part of the force of the track lies in Gavin's repetition, in her insistence. In a society that reliably tells Queer people that there's something not right about our desires, Gavin not only playfully enumerates her desires, but also emphatically declares, "There's nothing wrong with what I want."

It's worth mentioning something else the synth-saturated song reveals about Queer desire—the fact that it's often attended by a sense of belatedness.

Consider the pre-chorus. "I've spent way too many years not knowing what / What I wanted, how to get it, how to live it, and now / I'm gonna make up for it all at once / 'Cause that's, that's just what I want," Gavin sings.

The first time I heard those lines, I was struck by the familiarity of the notion of belatedness Gavin articulates. After I came out toward the end of college, I felt that I had lots to catch up on in terms of Queer socializing and intimacy. And I, too, wanted to make up for it—the range of experiences I'd been denied while in the closet—all at once.

Notably, "What I Want" isn't the first slice of pop culture to illuminate this particular dimension of missed opportunity. As I wrote for *Pacific Standard* (January 18, 2018), Luca Guadagnino's remarkable 2017 coming-of-age film *Call Me by Your Name* is "an exploration of the sometimes-heartrending ways in which time, whittled down by a nasty world, works against Queer people."

This gets me back to the "urgent" bit I nodded to earlier. "What I Want" comes at a tumultuous time, when many figures on the political right are once more weaponizing Queer people's desires against us and accusing us of social deviance. "What I Want" provides a moving rebuttal to the bogus claims being directed at Queer people—and serves as a reminder that there's nothing wrong with what we want.

Four Engines

Claire Whitehurst

Monotype with gouache and colored pencil on kozo paper, 2021
24" x 18"

Self-Portrait (An Echo)

Claire Whitehurst

Oil on linen, 2022
28" x 22"

Marching OUT in 1993

Judith Williams

Introduction

As I was unpacking after my move in 2021 to Greenville, South Carolina, I was pleasantly surprised to find a yellowed copy of an essay I had written in February of 1994 when I was a junior in college. "The March," crafted as an auto-ethnographic account, describes my experience at the March on Washington for Lesbian, Gay, and Bi Equal Rights and Liberation on April 25, 1993, one of the most memorable events of my life and an exquisitely glorious moment of activism. The transgressive cultural references in "The March"—such as "boom boxes" and the radical feminist linguistic symbolism of "womyn"—document Queer history through a Black feminist lens that makes this account intriguing and relevant. The narrative also underscores the impact of the AIDS epidemic and HIV on the Queer community in the 1990s.

On the day of the March, I recall getting lost quite often as we wandered the Mall, fascinated by colorful people and events. Looking back, I wonder how we navigated such a trip without cell phones or the internet. At the same time, I realize that the lack of digital distractions made the day even more poignant. We were completely engaged in the wonder of the experience, and somehow we felt free to *just be*, knowing that everyone would show up in the correct place at the appointed time—that everything would be all right.

What I didn't share in the original essay was that I ended up coming out to my family and friends because of events that happened that day. When it was our turn to march with the Rhode Island contingent, I provocatively stood behind the state banner with leaders of the delegation. Our photo was published in the *Providence Journal-Bulletin*, and by the time I returned home, word had spread throughout the restaurant where I worked that the rumors were true—I was indeed a lesbian. I never looked back. I moved to the South Beach neighborhood in Miami Beach, Florida, where I lived for the first time as an openly gay woman. A few years later, I adopted a child with my (then) lesbian partner. My child is now an adult who is non-binary and transgender. Almost thirty years later, I am still an activist, unfortunately fighting many of the same battles that led to that famous march. I am hopeful that by sharing a few of the personal experiences that have shaped me as a Queer Black college professor, I will not only help reduce some of the Queer phobias in academia (and beyond), but also help to normalize differences in our increasingly diverse world.

"The March" (1994)

I mulled it over in my mind several times that day. The kind of thing you do when you're indecisive. Should I or shouldn't I? Yes, it would be fun and exciting and for a good cause, but I was tired. It had been a long week. Things were hectic. It gets that way when you study full time and work three jobs. Anyway, my buddy Darin talked me into it. It was hard to say no to him. He was the type of guy who always came through for me when I needed special favors. You know, those pick-me-up-at-the-airport, watch-my-cat-for-the-weekend types of favors. Never mind the fact that he drank a little too much, collected *Simpsons* memorabilia, and had a wanna-be career in the film industry. He was funny. Funny in that special way that comes only from knowing how to laugh at yourself. His gaiety was a result of many things, but his humor came from the heart.

He eventually won me over with the "noble cause" routine. At least I preferred to think of it that way. It was for the cause and not for the promise of a twenty-four-hour party that convinced me to board that bus at midnight and head for Washington, D.C.

As bus trips go, this one wasn't too bad. At least I was on the smoking bus. I have this theory about smokers. They are the live-it-up, life's-too-short kinds of people. With a great sense of mortality, they know how to let their hair down and party. So, we rocked that bus until 6:00 in the morning, by which time most of us had slipped into a drunken semi-sleep. We dozed for the next couple of hours until we arrived at our destination.

As I disembarked, I began to feel the excitement in the air. The parking lot was filled with rows of buses unloading hundreds of people. Boom boxes were blaring the song, "We are Family." Vendors were hawking their merchandise: t-shirts, buttons, posters, flags, and stickers. There were sounds of loud laughter and jocularity. Waiting for the festivities to begin, I felt as anxious as a child in line for the ice cream truck.

Darin and I had made some new friends since the journey began. There was David the real estate agent. He was "pee-shy." He could urinate only in seclusion and as a result spent the last few hours on the bus with his eyeballs floating and his legs tightly crossed. Then there was "Pixie." His real name eludes me. He was a waif of a man. Maybe all of ninety pounds soaking wet. He had the type of milk-white skin that the Victorian virgins in Barbara Cartland's romance novels have. His hair and clothing were as black as midnight, which over-accentuated his pale skin and slight body. Last, but not least, there was Bill. He appeared rather non-descript and ordinary at first. He was balding, wore thick glasses, and talked only when spoken to. Well, first appearances can be deceiving. He emerged from the porta-potty a changed man. He was resplendent in flowered bell-bottoms, platform shoes, and a tight and oh-so-plunging t-shirt. His spectacles were replaced with some way-out shades. Suddenly, he seemed to have plenty to say.

Our small and diverse group made its way in search of a Bloody Mary and the Mall by heading toward that big phallic symbol (the Washington Monument). As we approached the Mall, we noticed that the crowd began to take on a certain "Queerness." Rainbow flags and pink triangles littered the air. Men strolled casually dressed in bridal gowns complete with veils or in stiletto heels with mini-skirts and exaggerated make-up. Bare-breasted "womyn" were everywhere in thongs or skirts or jeans. Some womyn wore leather riding pants and carried whips with studs or chains harnessed to their slaves. Martina Navratilova could be heard but not quite seen on a distant stage delivering her speech. Madonna, Phil Donahue, and Jesse Jackson were reported to be among the crowd.

We were all there for one primary reason. To make a statement, take a stand. We wanted to show our strength and unity en masse. We were there to march for equal and civil rights for gay, lesbian, and bisexual people. We were there to march for reproductive choice and freedom. We were there to demand an end to the military ban on homosexuals. We were there. One million of us strong. Gay, lesbian, straight, and bi. Black, white, Latin, and Asian. Parents, children, lovers, and friends. We wanted to tell America, "Get over it! Hate is not a family value. Straight does not mean narrow. Stop the bigotry." We had much to say. Hopefully someone would listen. Whether they did or not, we seized the moment to celebrate, appreciate, and tolerate our differences.

There were over one hundred groups marching that day. The diversity of their professional, social, regional, and ethnic backgrounds amazed me. People had come from as far away as Hawaii and Alaska. Even politicians showed up. While we waited for our contingent's turn to march (we were number seventy-six), we walked and gawked and talked. Sometimes we got lost among the vast and interesting crowd, ending up far from our contingent.

I thought about the people who had walked this turf before. I wondered what it was like at that last big civil rights march on the Mall. The one in the Sixties that called for an end to racial discrimination and segregation. The Sixties seems so long ago. It saddens me to think how little life has changed. Was I foolish to think that I could see a difference within my generation? Suddenly, I felt ready to march. I moved to the front of my contingent, held my placard high, posed for photographs, and led the way.

We saw the Pentagon, marched past the White House, and walked around the Mall. We were cheered on by festive supporters on the sidelines. We encountered only one group of demonstrators; we hooted and hollered Queer chants and jeers at them. As we approached the AIDS Memorial Quilt, a reverent silence fell over everybody. The music and dancing stopped. Loudspeakers no longer blared. As we started to read the patches, we began to hear sobs and weeping. I looked at my group of mostly newfound friends. We hugged. Then we, too, started to cry.

It was a quiet ride home late that night. No one said much of anything. To add to the somberness of our mood, one of the people on the bus who was HIV+ had collapsed during the day. He had been admitted to the hospital and would not be returning home with us.

I pondered over the events of the day. I was very glad that I had made the trip. I felt that I had made a significant contribution to history and social progress. I stood up for what I believed in. I wasn't just a talker—I was also a doer. My motivation and inner strength were heightened. I knew I could do anything.

I learned much from that trip. I learned about what was really important. VCRs, cellular phones, new cars, and fancy clothes don't count. The right of every individual to live their lives in dignity, to choose their own definition of family, and to have an equal opportunity to care for themselves—these are the things that are truly important.

CONTRIBUTORS

Elizabeth Allen is an elementary teacher in Greenville, South Carolina, who loves spending her days with third graders. She earned a B.A. and an M.A. in education from Furman University in 2020 and 2022, respectively. She lives with her three guinea pigs and one very loud cat.

Trevor Beeson is a pseudonym for a contributor who wishes to remain anonymous.

Robert Cain is a Greenville native who has worked in the nonprofit sector since graduating from Furman University in 2019 with a B.A. in economics. An avid traveler, he enjoys hiking and visiting new places. When not traveling, you will catch him watching the U.S. women's soccer team or playing with his nieces and nephews.

K.C. Cox is a senior custodial staff member at Furman University where he has worked for twenty-four years and served as a mentor for transgender students. He loves to fish, camp, cook, and has been active in Greenville's Julie Valentine Center. He lives by the motto, "I can't wait for what lies before me!"

Caroline Davis is a Visiting Lecturer in Theatre Arts at Furman University with a focus on new play development and dramaturgy. When not working on a production, she is usually watching tawdry reality television with her cat, Quincy.

Liv Fletcher is a sophmore at Furman University. She is majoring in education with the goal of becoming an elementary teacher. As the vice president of the Furman Pride Alliance, she aspires to make campus safer for Queer and transgender students. In her free time, she enjoys watching or reading any piece of Queer media she can find.

Mark Allan Gunnells loves to tell stories and receive reader feedback. This has been the case ever since he began penning one-page knockoffs of "Twilight Zone" episodes when he was a kid. He likes to think he has gotten a little better since then. He lives in Greer, South Carolina, with his husband, Craig A. Metcalf.

Kelsey Hample is an Assistant Professor of economics at Furman University. She studies human behavior in the context of low-income communities and loves sharing behavioral and development economics with her students. She is a general hobbyist who has recently enjoyed gardening and woodworking.

Benjamin Haywood is the Associate Director of the Faculty Development Center at Furman University where he provides direct support for a wide variety of programs, workshops, research efforts, and strategic initiatives. As a wildlife enthusiast, he enjoys hiking, birding, eco-travel, gardening, and spending time with his dog, Harmony.

A. Scott Henderson is the William R. Kenan Jr. Professor of Education at Furman University. Born and raised in South Florida, he is an animal lover who likes to paint, play the trumpet, and write poetry/short stories.

Riley Hughes is currently the Post-Baccalaureate Fellow for Furman University's Women's, Gender, and Sexuality Studies (WGSS) program. As a Queer woman who struggles with mental health issues, her passions include intersectional feminist studies and mental health advocacy. After serving as the WGSS Fellow, she will begin pursuing an M.A. in Higher Education with a focus on Diversity and Social Justice in Higher Education at the University of Michigan.

Kevin Kao is an Assistant Professor of Art at Furman University. Born and raised in California, he is a sculptor who explores the construction of collective identity through figure, reflection, and multiplicity. His work has been exhibited in numerous venues, including the Crocker Art Museum in Sacramento and the Kranzberg Arts Center in St. Louis. He was a 2021 finalist in the Young Sculptors Competition at Miami University, and has received grants from the Regional Arts Commission in St. Louis and the Northern Clay Center in Minneapolis. He earned a B.S. in Biology from the University of California, San Diego, and an M.F.A. in Studio Art from the University of Tennessee, Knoxville.

Nick Radel is a Professor of English at Furman University. He has been writing about and teaching LGBTQIA+ literature and theory, as well as courses in diversity, equity, and inclusion, since the mid-1980s. These are his first efforts at fiction or autofiction.

Roger A. Sneed is a Professor of Religion and Chair of the Faculty at Furman University. He is the author of *The Dreamer and the Dream: Afrofuturism and Black Religious Thought* (2021). He is a devout Trekkie and inordinately proud of the Geek Shrine in his Furman office.

Brandon Tensley is a journalist in Washington, D.C., covering culture, identity, and politics. He earned an M.A. in politics from the University of Oxford and a B.A. in German studies and political science from Furman University. He is a Whitney Houston superfan.

Claire Whitehurst is the current Artist in Residence at Furman University. Born in Baton Rouge, Louisiana, she is a painter, printmaker, and sculptor who draws from the physical and emotional landscape of the Deep South, exploring Queer narrative, memory, time, and identity through color, form, surface, and environment. She holds an M.F.A. in painting from the University of Iowa and a B.F.A. from the University of Mississippi. She was a Stanley Fellow at the University of Iowa in 2018, which provided her with the opportunity to study cave paintings and engravings in southern France. Her research focused on the relationship between surface and image, and the nuances of abstract narrative. Her work has been exhibited nationally and internationally, and a book of her drawings and writings was published in 2021 through Drum Machine Editions in Asheville, North Carolina. Her work has been published in *New American Paintings*, *Oxford American*, and *ArtMaze Magazine*, among many others.

Judith Williams is an Assistant Professor of Anthropology at Furman University. A former chef and caterer, she studies race and gender hierarchies in restaurant labor. After coming out at the March on Washington for Lesbian, Gay, and Bi Equal Rights and Liberation in 1993, she became involved in Queer rights activism in Miami, Florida. She continues to be a passionate advocate for the most marginalized members of the LGBTQIA+ community.

ACKNOWLEDGMENTS

This book would not have been possible without the talents, insights, and patience of the contributors. They have shared their reflections about the past, their challenges with the present, and their hopes for the future. They have done so with candor that requires exceptional courage. The community that the contributors have helped to create—and continue to sustain—is a precious and valued resource.

We also owe thanks to the faculty, staff, and administrators of Furman University for their commitment to diversity, equity, and inclusive excellence. That commitment is "embodied by both [the] implicit values and explicit practices" of the institution. The production of this book was funded in part by a William R. Kenan Jr.-endowed professorship at Furman.

The editor would like to express special gratitude for the assistance and wise counsel of Jill Hendrix and Vally Sharpe of Fiction Addiction Publishing Services. Their attention to detail is commendable and much appreciated.

Finally, we gratefully acknowledge the support (and forbearance) of colleagues, family, friends, and animal companions. You know who you are.